DRAWING AND PAINTING ARCHITECTURE

TOWN HOUSE.
WINCHESTER.
Ray Evans

DRAWING AND PAINTING ARCHITECTURE *Ray Evans*

VNR VAN NOSTRAND REINHOLD COMPANY
NEW YORK   CINCINNATI   TORONTO   LONDON   MELBOURNE

Published by Van Nostrand Reinhold Company Inc.
135 West 50th Street
New York, New York 10020

Library of Congress Catalog Card Number 83–6491
ISBN 0–442 – 22197–5 cloth
        0–442 – 22196–7 paper

Produced by Bettina Tayleur Ltd
1 Newburgh Street, London W1V 1LH

Typeset in Palatino by Input Typesetting Ltd, London
Color reproduction by Bright Arts (Hong Kong) Ltd,
and printed and bound in Italy by Sagdos SpA, Milan,
for Imago Publishing Ltd

Designed by Tim Higgins

Library of Congress Cataloging in Publication Data

Evans, Ray
        Drawing and painting architecture.
        Bibliography: p.
        includes index.
        1. Buildings in art. 2. Art—Technique. 3. Building.
        4. Architecture—Terminology. I. Title.
        N8217.B85E9 1983   751.4   83–6491
        ISBN 0–442–22197–5
        ISBN 0–442–22196–7 (pbk.)

To Angela, Bettina, Cathy and Keith

Acknowledgements

I would like to thank the following for their help and
encouragement in the preparation of this book:
Anthony Eyre, Art for Offices, Bettina Tayleur, Cathy
Gosling, Tim Higgins, Keith and Carol Leaman, Tina
Rogers and Simon Young.

For the reproduction of their paintings and the loan of
colour transparencies of some of these I would like to
thank:
Dalgetty Spillers (Frontispiece); Deloitte, Haskins and
Sells (pp. 144, 147); Foyles Book Club (pp. 92–3);
F. P. Gintz Esq (p. 108); A. E. Gordon Esq (p. 107);
Rosemary Gould (pp. 84–5, 116–7); J. Leek Esq (p. 86);
Letraset International (p. 17); Rex Mead (pp. 44, 134–5);
Royles Publications, 1983 Abbey National Calendar
(Frontispiece and pp. 17, 19, 48, 68, 86); Michael Sidey
(p. 88); Simon Young (p. 48).

For the reproduction of drawings I would like to thank:
Consumers Association, for drawings in *The Good Hotel
Guide* (pp. 91, 129); the Countryman Magazine (pp. 90,
110–11, 118–19); Hamble Point Marina (pp. 84–5);
Hampshire County Council (p. 134); Paris, Smith and
Randall (pp. 124, 146); Royles Publications, Abbey
National Calendar (pp. 16, 49).

Contents

Introduction   7

Know Your Own House   10

Some American Sketches   29

First Approaches   38

Equipment and Materials   51

Field and Studio Work   64

Pictures for the Market Place   81

Buildings in Their Environment   97

Panoramic Paintings   126

Presenting Your Work   145

Conclusion   151

Glossary of Architectural Terms   152

Bibliography   156

Index   159

Sketching is very closely bound up with travelling and discovering new subjects, such as this striking church tower at Mont Dol in France.

Introduction

Can anyone draw buildings without knowing something about their construction and history? I doubt it, any more than the human figure can be drawn without a knowledge of anatomy. The stimulation of interest in buildings grows as one becomes more aware of their personalities and the reasons behind their construction, and there is no better way of understanding the technical and aesthetic qualities of architecture than by learning to draw it.

Buildings have a life of their own, passing from bright youth through majestic and mature middle age, and sometimes on into stages of decay – often the most interesting to the artist.

My personal involvement with architecture began in the 1930s when I was learning the profession of architect in an office in North Wales, and the discipline of drawing for construction has always stayed with me. Later, during the Second World War, I determined to become an artist and learnt the expressive side of drawing as well as the use of sketchbooks. For many years good accurate drawing was despised in the art schools, but now I am glad to see it returning to favour.

A keen observant draughtsman will draw anything with understanding but I have found that an architectural training has been especially useful in drawing buildings. It helps you to interpret what you see, and also to know about the things you cannot see. This knowledge is invaluable when working up subjects from photographs or quick sketches, and gives the artist the comfortable freedom of the studio as well as the exciting but sometimes inconvenient experience of working out of doors.

It is sometimes hard to see whether a finished studio picture is really an improvement on a quick sketch made on the site in the enthusiasm of finding a new subject. Many artists and collectors prefer the sketches, even if, like mine, they are sometimes covered with written notes. Artists of the past like Turner and Constable often seem to have had their best moments working on a small scale under the immediate influence of a subject or landscape. Many amateurs seldom pass beyond this enjoyable notebook stage, but there are challenges and opportunities in larger scale and more reflective work which should tempt most sketchers to try studio work as well.

All the drawings in this book have some kind of story or anecdote attached to them, and the happy coincidence of travel, work and the discovery of wonderful buildings happens all the time. As a typical instance, the drawing of a barn in Connecticut (*opposite*) was the result of a lucky find, and it may help to explain my working methods in a

An old barn in Connecticut.

quick *resumé* by describing this drawing and how it came to be done.

It was in April 1982 that I was staying with friends near Essex, Connecticut and mentioned to them the fine barns that I had seen while driving up through Pennsylvania. The snow had prevented me from stopping on the road, but I hoped that they might know of one nearby which I could draw. My hosts took me twelve miles away to Haddam, and there we found this magnificent structure.

It was the biggest barn I had ever seen, or even imagined – at least seventy feet to the weather vanes on top of the two cupolas which bestrode the ridge of the roof. These served as ventilators, but as I discovered from Eric Sloane's *The Age of Barns* the farmers soon began to develop their own style of design, so that from their origins as functional buildings, the barns began to be conscious works of architecture. (Later, on a trip to see the barn, my editor found out that the cupolas had been made by a retired ship's carpenter.) On the northern side, hard against the barn, stood two great cylindrical silos which may have been added near the end of the last century. They were topped with double sloped octagonal roofs clad in wooden shingles, and each had a dormer window facing outwards. The silos penetrated deep into the ground and were clad with large glazed ceramic tiles in deep orange and brown. The wooden planks of the building were painted dark blood red, and were peeling from exposure to the sun.

The building was as huge as a cinema, but had the grace of a French chateau. There was no one about, so we began to investigate more closely. In its former use, the hay must have been hoisted to the upper level for storage through two huge doors which, judging by the position of the hinges, swung downwards from the apex of the gable end of the roof; the remains of the hoist were visible outside. The lower part inside was now used as a garage and workshop, but here the cattle lived in the winter, and there were signs of an overhead cable mechanism for carrying away manure. A walk round the outside took some time because of the huge size, and the remains of large snowdrifts from the previous week. After an hour of peering through very dirty windows and speculating on what certain vents and openings were for and patting its worn wooden planking as if it was a great animal, I knew it was something I must draw. The next day I made a two-hour study, illustrated here, from my car. With the car door open I had a good view and was out of the wind.

My American sketchbook was filled with different types of paper, about the same size as this book. For this subject I chose a David Cox paper, yellow ochre in colour with a rough surface. The work began with a careful outline drawing of the silhouette of the building, starting with the metal cow on the centre weather-vane. At this stage it is vital to get the scale right, so as to prevent the infuriating discovery, half way through, that there is no room for the foreground. Before long, it was time for some colour – applied from a miniature travelling box with a limited range of colours squeezed fresh out of the watercolour tubes for each outing. On this occasion I had brought alizarin brown madder, warm sepia, prussian blue, lamp black and raw sienna. Two good sable brushes were all that was necessary for applying the colour.

The roofs were washed in with warm grey over

8

the top of the cupolas – prussian blue with sepia and a touch of black. After this came a red wash for the walls (brown madder with a little blue and black). The work was then pressed lightly with blotting paper, a valuable device for speeding drying and giving texture, lifting the colour off the raised surface of the paper and deepening the colour in the hollows.

After this, the details had to be given individuality. In a wash of raw sienna over the barn and silos, some tiles were picked out in pen, and the windows were left blank, while the base of the building was washed in a darker colour, and then the pen was used again for the tiles, the window panes and general strengthening. The winter trees and the foreground grass were also best done in pen. At this point the whole work needed pulling together, and this was done with a heavy wash of blue black shadow over roof, building and foreground together. This was blotted when half dry and I added some finishing touches of bright colour on the barn and white gouache to highlight the towers (even in the shade) and the window frames and snowdrift against the yellow paper. With a few more touches of the pen, the drawing was complete.

This example introduces some of the subjects covered in this book, through which I hope you will share my enjoyment in studying buildings and drawing them. Every part of a building has a story – a walled-up door or window, a crack in the stonework or the succession of small alterations made by successive owners. As many painters of the past have discovered, buildings can be as eloquent and evocative as waterfalls, lakes or trees. Nor is it only picturesque buildings – pretty little thatched cottages or gate lodges to parks – which make good drawings. The industrial scenery of the great manufacturing towns, the skyscrapers of New York and almost anything in the generous sunlight of the Mediterranean make good subjects, and this is only the beginning of the exploration.

The more you paint, the more you start looking, and buildings you have passed by for years without noticing suddenly, in a particular light or weather, become subjects for pictures. Once you have learnt the technique, you need not be afraid of tackling anything, large or small – everything from a city to a garden wall is interesting to an architectural painter. Because I believe that knowledge of building construction helps you to see things as they really are, I have begun this book with an anatomy of building, taking the structure apart to show how it has been put together. Techniques and materials are a personal matter, but passing on information from one enthusiast to another is always valuable, and it is worth having a shot at all the techniques which might help you to get closer to your subject. Over and above the ever-intriguing business of buying new paints, pens and pencils is the actual selection of subject matter which you find exciting. It is up to the individual to develop his or her own style; but I hope that the wide range of subjects represented in the latter part of the book will stimulate you to new efforts. Perhaps you will stop in your tracks one day and say, 'That's a Ray Evans subject', but I hope you will not draw it for that reason alone. Find things which speak directly to you and then all the manifold difficulties of sitting on a rickety stool for hours in wind or rain, bothered by passers-by or missing the last train home, will vanish like magic.

A quick line drawing in the field: the Café du Quai in Dieppe.

Know Your Own House

Although our lives are lived in and around buildings, few of us pay much attention to their actual structure and construction. All too often you learn about the essentials of building design when there happens to be something wrong with the particular design you are living in, and a roof has to be mended, or walls secured from damp. One is more likely to have some passing appreciation of architectural decoration, but this knowledge can only be enriched if it is based on an understanding of the history and techniques of building. The best building to start looking at is the one which will be most familiar, the one in which you live. While you may never have considered your home as serious architecture, it will probably embody design principles and building techniques which have a long history and can be found in many older buildings.

Our house in Winchester was originally a farmhouse, built almost two hundred years ago, before the railway from London caused the city to grow. Although it is small, it has the generous proportions which Georgian builders seem to have grasped instinctively, so that the same design would still look right if enlarged. In a district of Victorian houses with slate roofs, our red tiles stand out, and the old farm buildings, now used by a monumental mason and sculptor, run along beside the house.

Looking at the drawing opposite, you can see the brick quoins (pillars built into the wall) at each corner of the facade, and the line of brick lacing courses running across the middle supporting the timber floor joists inside. There are stone lintels, quoins and sills to the sliding sash windows, but otherwise the walls are built with knapped (split) flints laid in courses with wide mortar joints in a traditional method known as flintwalling. An opportunity of going behind the surface arose recently when a crack opened up in the flintwalling, a delayed reaction to subsidence in 1911. A surprising discovery was that, instead of rising from a broad foundation, the walls actually tapered to a point about two feet below ground level, resting directly on the chalk, as was common practice at the time. In order to underpin the affected area, we took down the outside skin of the wall, revealing an inside wall made of brick rubble and flints – in hardly any house does the material seen on the outside penetrate all the way through the wall. The final layer beyond the inside wall, common to most houses not built of stone, is the original lath and plaster. It was a fascinating voyage of exploration into the unseen core of the house.

In the drawing of the house certain details have been enlarged to show the way in which the components have been assembled:

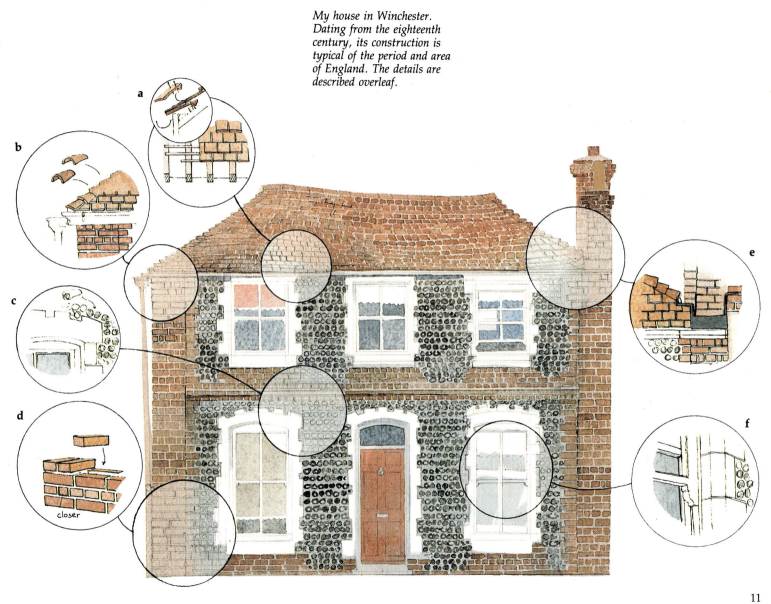

My house in Winchester. Dating from the eighteenth century, its construction is typical of the period and area of England. The details are described overleaf.

a

b

c

d

closer

e

f

11

(a) The roof is constructed on a timber frame, with hipped (sloped) ends. There are purlins (running across the sloping faces), rafters (running up and down) and vertical posts supporting the triangular frame. Laths are battened across on which to hang the clay tiles, as shown here. These tiles overlap, giving a thickness of three tiles at each join. Old tiles tend to have an irregular look, especially if, as here, they have been lifted off and replaced on a rebuilt roof. These flat tiles are characteristic of Winchester and the south of England; as one moves away to other parts of the country one finds the larger, wavy pantiles, slates varying in thickness and colour depending on where they have been quarried, and wooden shingles. These are all hung by the same method, with nails going into the laths. Clay tiles also have projecting nibs to hang over the laths.

(b) The junction of the two faces of the roof calls for a different shape of tile, as does the top ridge. The gutter is fixed to a fascia board, which in turn is attached to an unseen timber, the wall plate, which lies on top of the wall and supports the roof timbers. This simple roof is all ridges, the opposite of which are all valleys, and allow for the most difficult demonstration of the tiler's art, the swept valley with specially made angle tiles interlocking where the two sloping faces meet at an internal angle.

(c) A speciality of English chalk counties like Hampshire is flint construction; the flints had to be cleared off the fields, and were the only local hard stone. They are irregularly shaped lumps of silica, formed through the fossilization of sponges, and, although difficult to shape to requirements, they are unique among building materials for their hard

and glittering texture. The mediaeval church-builders of East Anglia realized their artistic possibilities in their beautiful flushwork patterns at the base of towers and porches. In this case, the flints were split and laid lengthwise running back into the wall like large teeth, with the thin end pointing inwards. The egg-shaped heads at the outer end were cut square to give a glassy black face with a white rind set into white mortar. Because of their weight and irregularity, only five courses of flints can be laid in a day while the mortar is setting. Window openings and angles need extra reinforcement in some other material, and so the windows here are given stone surrounds. The lintel (on top) and the sill (below) are each made of a whole piece of stone, but notice how the ground floor lintels are cut in a pattern to imitate the quoins (alternately broad and narrow) of the jambs (literally legs, the sides of the window and door frames). This irregular shape also helps to give an interlocking grip with the flint wall, and the brick quoins at the angles are treated in the same way.

(d) Bricks, the commonest British building material, only make a guest appearance here, partly concealed underground in the new foundations, and otherwise confined to the chimney and angles. They are also used in the lacing courses which serve to strengthen the flintwalling. Most bricks are a standard size, adapted to what will comfortably fit a bricklayer's hand. When laid across the face of the wall with their long side showing they are called stretchers; if laid the other way, they are called headers. Alternating courses of these, as seen here, have the name English bond, one of many bonds used in brick laying, which are illustrated later.

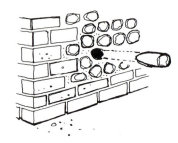

Flintwalling: flints are set in mortar, pointed end inwards.

Two traditional types of wood frame: the cruck frame and the box frame.

(e) Back on the roof again, brick meets tile, and the junction is created with a sheet of pliable lead, tucked into the brickwork and under the tiles like an apron. Large 'flats' on a roof were traditionally covered in lead, an asset too valuable in some cases for thieves, (or even owners) to leave it undisturbed.

(f) The wooden frames of the sash windows are recessed some way into the wall of the house, with the jambs cut with a chamfered angle to let more light in directly or by reflection. This depth, and the different planes of the two sashes (the upper always overlapping the lower) are important and often ignored considerations when drawing a building.

Here, then, is my house, and I hope you will be encouraged to take a closer look at your own, and indeed all buildings you come across, whether old or new, to see why they are built in their different ways.

From the earliest times house construction relied on available materials and their natural properties. Wood was probably the earliest used material, being generally available and easy to work; in the United States and other countries with large forests, such as Russia and Scandinavia, the log cabin is a typical type of early building, remaining popular to this day.

There are two main types of wood frame house which have a long history, the cruck frame, with its wishbone-shaped legs, and the box frame, suited to lighter, straighter timbers. It was a very adaptable system, for the windows could be placed where required, and opened up or walled in at will, and the wall-filling, whether of wattle and daub or other flexible materials, carried no weight and thus could move and breathe with the building. A thatched roof was very light, and gave good insulation, although it was also a fire hazard. Barring such accidents, these houses get stronger with age and should last for ever. The timber frame was usually plastered over for protection. Its exposure and painting in black was a Victorian romantic affectation which is still with us, although some of the great timbered Tudor mansions of Cheshire, like Moreton Old Hall, have a giant zebra effect which must have been intended to be seen. In East Anglia and elsewhere the plaster was decorated

Below left A house in Burford, in the Cotswolds, built on a traditional box frame.

Wattle and daub, the method of walling which is most common to a wood frame house.

13

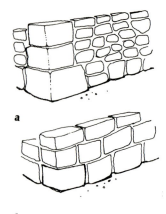

a

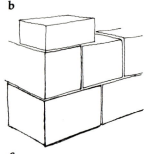

b

c

a Random shaped stones with quoins built of larger, squarer stones for strength. b Dressed stones, chipped into shape by hand. c Ashlar – stones sawn into shape by a mason.

with elaborate patterns incised or built up in a relief method called pargetting, which with luck may escape too violent a pink colourwash from modern paint.

Methods of walling like cob (clay with sand, gravel and straw) and rammed earth or *pisé de terre* have very ancient origins, and can still be seen in many English houses. Cob is a speciality of Devon, giving rise to those characteristic bulging walls with very small deep window openings. The old saying is that if a cob wall has a good hat and a good pair of shoes, it will last for centuries. The hat is usually a thatched roof, and the shoes must be a dry and impermeable foundation, and then the saying is quite true. *Pisé* is usually rendered over so that it is not immediately detectable from the outside, but a tumbledown cottage or one being restored will sometimes reveal examples of this type of wall which has to be built up inside a wooden shuttering and rammed into place. Rammed earth construction can often be found wherever clay is readily available; as I describe later on, in South Carolina I stayed in a house built by this method.

Other ancient types of wall were built of stones, usually taken off fields or out of stream beds and used in their original shape. If you study a dry-stone wall (without mortar) you will see the skill which goes into selecting exactly the right stone to lie comfortably with its neighbours. For houses, the gaps would be filled with earth. Slate and limestone, however, can easily be worked into shapes which will lie in regular courses on the face of the wall and resist the weather better. The large solid stones would then be shaped for the corners as quoins.

For important buildings in the middle ages, stone would be transported (most easily by water) from a good quarry and shaped into more solid regular courses, although these stones would still probably be plastered over and colourwashed. Most European cathedrals were like this, continuing a tradition deriving from classical times. In the nineteenth century the colour was removed in the belief that if the builders had used stone, they must have wanted it to be seen. Behind the face of the wall, and often in less important parts of the exterior, the older method of random rubble was still used.

There were, indeed, occasions when the stone was meant to show on the outside, but it would then usually be dressed (smoothed and squared up) and laid in even more regular lines.

When stone has been cut and shaped to give it a perfectly smooth and regular finish, with hardly any space in the joints, the term ashlar is used. Stones used in this way, if they are of a sedimentary kind like limestone, have to face the same point of the compass that they did in the quarry bed, otherwise they will erode much faster. The other mysterious property of stone is that often, immediately after it has come out of the quarry, it can be carved and shaped with the ease of butter. It takes some time to develop a hard skin and seasons gradually like timber. Thus stone, although proverbially hard, is as much a living material as wood, and the mason's skill lies in extracting its best qualities. Once in place, it will weather differently according to the amount of sunlight it receives, while the design of mouldings and projections influences the way in which water runs down the facade or bounces off it. Mouldings, as the ancient Greeks discovered, also have an aes-

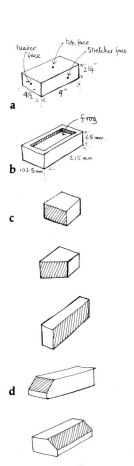

thetic purpose in creating the modulation of light and shade on curved and flat surfaces.

Bricks are not generally held to be so romantic as stone, nor so grand. There is the famous story of King George III visiting a house in Dorset in 1794, which had been built for the owner's grandfather seventy years before. All the King could find to say was 'Brick, Mr Pitt, brick', after which, at great cost, the facades were covered with Portland stone. Nonetheless, bricks have a long history, originally used throughout Europe by the Romans, who shaped them like tiles, and laid them in long thin courses. These Roman bricks can occasionally be found re-used in later buildings.

Only in the late middle ages did bricks reappear, originating from the Netherlands. Soon they were produced in a number of countries, standard sizes being introduced in the sixteenth century. The sizes have varied over the years, and are a useful way of dating a wall. The colours also vary from rich red to pale yellow, the latter being popular to imitate the effect of stone. There are also purple engineering bricks, glazed headers for decoration, and glazed ceramic bricks in many colours. In the nineteenth century these were often used in combination with moulded terracotta to create what was called permanent polychromy. There is a difference between stock bricks like the rather anaemically coloured Flettons, designed to be used unseen on the inside of a wall, and facing bricks with a specially coloured surface. Architects can specify whether they want bricks picked out for uniform effect, or whether they want a deliberately varied wall where the bricks show the accidents of firing. Bricks can be cut and shaped by the expert hands of the bricklayer for the various functional

a Wire-cut brick; b pressed brick. c Half bat, bevelled bat and half-bat cut lengthwise. d Plinth header, plinth stretcher and bullnose.

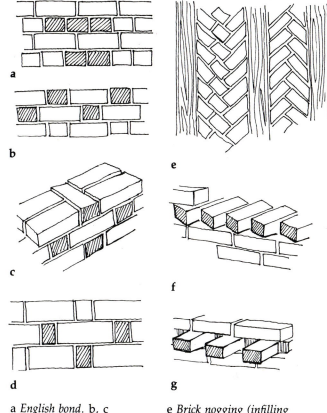

a English bond. b, c Flemish bond. d Chinese or rat-trap bond, the bricks laid on their sides.

e Brick nogging (infilling within a timber frame) in a herring-bone pattern. f and g bricks laid at an angle.

Wedge shaped bricks used on window and door surrounds. A wooden lintel behind usually carries the weight.

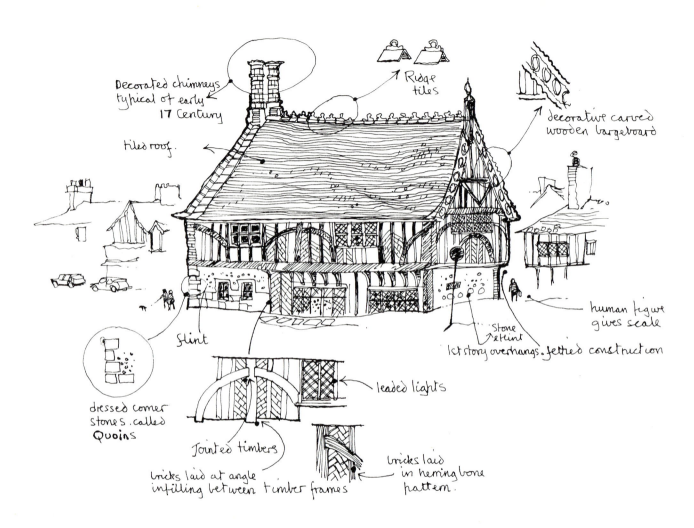

Decorated chimneys typical of early 17 Century

tiled roof.

Ridge tiles

decorative carved wooden bargeboard

human figure gives scale

Stone & flint

1st story overhangs. Jettied construction

Flint

dressed corner stones. called **Quoins**

Jointed timbers

leaded lights

bricks laid at angle infilling between timber frames

bricks laid in heringbone pattern.

The Moot Hall at Aldeburgh, Suffolk. This seventeenth-century box frame building makes a fascinating subject and introduces one to many interesting details, such as the decorated chimneys and carved wooden bargeboard.

The Moot Hall
Aldeburgh

Ray Evans Sept 80

and decorative purposes shown in the diagrams.

In forested areas, other methods of finishing walls were extensively used, such as wooden tile hanging, which is light but weatherproof and offers scope for decoration in the shaped end of the tiles. Slates can be hung in the same way. Wooden clapboard is a favourite device for farm buildings and the upper floors of houses, and is the most widespread method for covering the walls of timber houses in the United States. Nowadays the appearance of wooden clapboard is often successfully imitated by aluminium.

In the south of England, and occasionally elsewhere, the interesting eighteenth-century expedient of the mathematical tile, designed to give the appearance of brickwork to a wooden-framed house, can be detected, but usually only when one is chipped or broken, or when, for economy, the treatment did not extend round the corners of the house. This was one of the many devices of the late Georgian period to make buildings appear to be other than they really were, the commonest device being stucco (plaster or cement) rendering on brick, grooved and jointed like stone, and then painted with an oil paint in a stone colour. There were also artificial stone ornaments, most notably

In old buildings brick walls will often tend to bulge, and braces such as these will be bolted through them in order to strengthen them.

the English Coade Stone, which was cast by a cement process according to a secret and never rediscovered recipe, and has lasted better than the real thing in places like Bedford Square in London.

I have already looked at roofing tiles on the houses in Winchester and mentioned stone slates in passing. These give rise to especially fine building work as they are graded in size from top to bottom of the roof. As is usual in vernacular building, the reasons for this are partly functional and partly aesthetic. By putting large slates at the bottom of the roof there is a saving of labour, and by putting small ones at the top there is a reduction in weight, but no one could look at such a roof and say that it was not also done to give pleasure to the eye. Slaters have picturesque names for the different sizes – Duchesses, Marchionesses, Countesses – showing how the building materials were treated as though they had a personality of their own.

In the United States and Scandinavia wooden shingle roofs are common, and their revival in the 1880s for the large seaside 'cottages' of Rhode Island gave the name 'shingle style' to these attractively sprawling houses. Aluminium and lead are usually found on flat roofs, or used as flashing round chimneys and gutters. The tin roof, or corrugated iron roof, although a poor man's substitute for the traditional methods of roofing, can make good subject matter for drawing, particularly when partly rusted, and casting a wavy line shadow onto a wall below. In the late-nineteenth-century expansion of American towns the industrial methods of mass production were applied to building and pressed tin was used for a number of architectural ornaments, while whole buildings were bolted together from cast-iron sections.

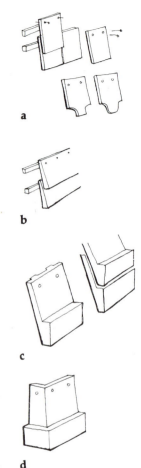

a

b

c

d

Wooden tiles and clapboarding (a and b) are a common alternative to brick. The mathematical tile (c, and a corner tile, d) was invented in the eighteenth century.

There are many variations on the basic tent-shape of a wooden-framed roof. In a cruck house, the roof and the wall are part of the same structure (see page 12). In the more complicated roofs every piece has its name, and for churches and great halls the hammer beam was discovered as a way of opening out the space inside the roof, and as a vehicle for decoration. When the roof space was needed for living quarters, the mansard, or double sloped roof was invented and popularized in France. The American version, with the gables cut square, is called a gambrel roof.

For chimneys, brick is a natural material because it is fireproof, and can be built to give a leakproof flue. Square and rectangular shapes are the most common, but round chimneys occur, especially in areas of rough stone like the west of Ireland, and the bricklayers of the sixteenth and seventeenth centuries enjoyed inventing fantastic hexagonal, octagonal and spiral designs, with decorated brick tops, projecting bricks, and staggered angles for weather protection.

The character of a house is often determined by the height and position of its chimneys, although it is unusual now to see smoke coming out of the

Bedford Square in London.

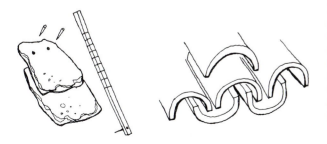

Far left, *stone flags, used to this day in England in the Cotswolds, with a measuring rod used to divide up the flags into their different sizes.* Left *Roman tiles, still the normal method of roofing in the Mediterranean.*

pots. Look at a house built only for central heating, or one where the chimneys have deliberately been removed and you will see that it is like looking at a face without a nose.

Architectural metalwork provides much interest for the painter, and lead gutters and rainwater heads (often with the date of the house and initials on them) give way in later decades to cast-iron balconies, porches and verandas. These were

19

construction of ridge tiles easily seen against sky.

traditional ridge tile.

Greeny tinge on tiles & bricks is from moss & lichen on north side of house

Details of cornices more easily seen against the sky, than on the nearer corner.

tile hung wall.

Note the decorative arch.

Notice how brick colour changes to a more yellow brick.

Details of brickwork both drawn & painted showing alternating header & stretchers

Beautiful window light, obscured by tree.

Sash windows
top window slides outside
bottom window

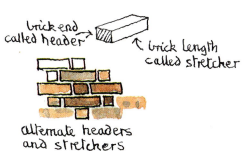

MANSARD
roof

brick end
called header

brick length
called stretcher

alternate headers
and stretchers
Flemish bond

This Georgian town house (opposite; see also frontispiece) dates from about 1800, and is a good example of the influence of the architect Henry Holland in its fine proportions and use of simple decoration.

Left *Details common to eighteenth-century architecture: above, sash windows, middle, the mansard or gambrel roof, and below, bricks laid in the Flemish bond.*

Two basic types of roof construction: the arched roof and the vaulted roof.

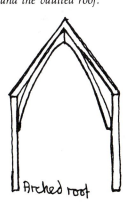

Arched roof

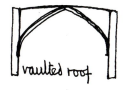

vaulted roof

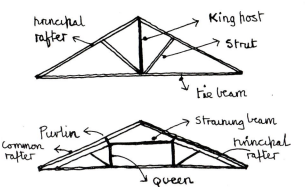

principal rafter   King host   Strut   tie beam

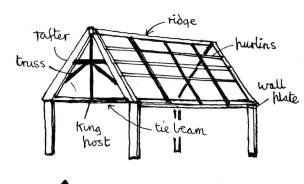

Purlin   straining beam   principal rafter   common rafter   queen

ridge   rafter   purlins   truss   wall plate   King host   tie beam

Wood frame roof construction, showing the parts common to most wood frame roofs and the principle of the hammer beam roof.

clearly designed not only to give shelter to the doors and windows, but to cast delicate filigree shadows on the face of the smooth brick or stucco walls. In the United States their place is sometimes taken by elegantly fretted wooden ornament.

Windows, the eyes in the face of a building, are also important in determining its character, and any drawing of a building will win or lose according to whether they are given a convincing treatment. Before the use of glass was common, while houses still had to consider their defensive role, domestic windows were small, narrow, lancet-type openings, although churches went from glory to glory in devising forms of tracery and designs in stained glass. In timber-framed houses, windows naturally spread horizontally, but in brick houses narrow tall openings were more practical, and accorded with the classical proportions of the Renaissance. The triumph of transparency can be seen in that Derbyshire prodigy house, Hardwick Hall, 'more glass than wall', built by a contemporary of Elizabeth I, Elizabeth, Countess of Shrewsbury, known as Bess of Hardwick.

In early windows the glazing was not made to open, and a wooden shutter was swung back above

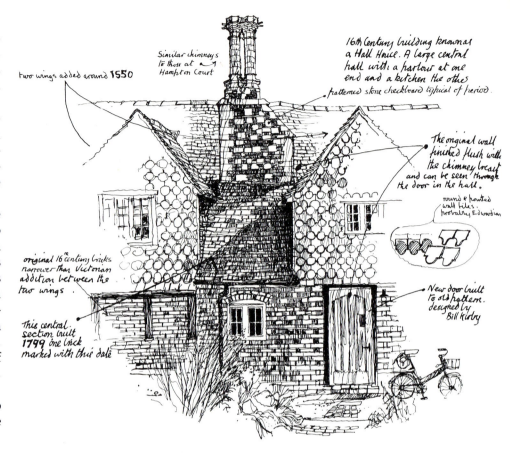

Similar chimneys to these at Hampton Court

two wings added around **1550**

16th Century building known as a Hall House. A large central hall with a parlour at one end and a kitchen the other

flattened stone checkboard typical of period

The original wall finished flush with the chimney breast and can be seen through the door in the hall

round & pointed wall tiles probably Edwardian

original 16th century bricks narrower than Victorian addition between the two wings.

This central section built **1799** one brick marked with this date

New door built to old pattern designed by Bill Kirby

A round chimney built of rough stone, typical to the west of Ireland.

it to give ventilation. The casement window, with a panel of leaded glass in a wooden frame opening outwards like a door, followed from this, but was necessarily limited in size. The sash window, best adapted for a vertical opening and consisting of two counterweighted wooden frames sliding in grooves, grew in popularity from 1700 and remained the standard British window for over a century, and one of our most enduring architec-

Abbot's Barton Farmhouse. This large timber frame farmhouse combines many interesting features, the main parts dating from the sixteenth and eighteenth centuries. The original building is made up of a hall with a parlour at one end and a kitchen at the other; the various later additions use a variety of materials. On the west front left the sixteenth-century stone checkboard pattern below the chimneys blends well with the early twentieth-century wall tiles covering the two gables. Below the various shapes of brick in the wall point to different centuries of building. The east front right provides an interesting contrast, its classical proportions typical of the Queen Anne period in which it was built. The porch is a Victorian addition, its pointed arch typical of the gothic revival.

16th Century barn.

Top windows originally same size as those below, half bricked in to improve proportion. (supposedly)

Walls on each side original 16th Century

Front porch is Victorian

These were never windows, as main wall of kitchen splits them. But brickwork suggests there should be windows to balance opposite side,

tural exports to the New World. Other European countries generally continued to use the casement, in combination with internal and external shutters. The early Georgian love of neatness and sparkle dictated that windows should be painted in the brightest white lead paint, and although the romantic period favoured richer and deeper colours, the revival of the use of white at the turn of the century has stayed with us as the natural colour against any wall surface.

Most eighteenth-century glass is crown glass, spun in a disc on the end of a rod, and possessing a slight unevenness of surface which gives life and sparkle to windows which have not been reglazed. The process also produced the bull's eye or knob of glass of the kind which is now carefully reproduced for use in modern Georgian houses which want to look antique. Originally this would have

many of these attractive ridge tiles were missing claytiled roof.

These dormers are newly added not on original building.

The diamond brickwork is interesting. A bricklayer explained to me that the blue bricks would be laid very carefully course by course to make the pattern, would be very costly today. (see notes about these dark bricks)

To be sure of the correct proportion of height to width I made the width of each tower ⅛ th the height. Having fixed this width

The Old Grammar School, Wimborne. This interesting Victorian building, built in 1851, was being converted into flats when I painted it, but the interesting facade was being cleverly retained; one of the few additions are the unobtrusive dormers on the roof. I sketched in the roof line and two towers with a conté charcoal pencil, adding a watercolour wash of brown madder alizarin and a touch of black over most of the building except for the window areas, using a No 6 brush. The ends of the building were drawn in charcoal and washed over with grey. The details were drawn in freely with a Gillott 290 nib and indian ink, serving to pull the sketch together. I find that using a colour wash before detailed penwork helps to keep a drawing free. Finally I picked out the details of stone and brick-work with a No 4 brush and burnt sienna.

be sure of being able to get the whole width across my two pages.

been sold off cheaply, melted down or thrown away. Perfectly smooth plate glass could not be manufactured commercially until the mid-nineteenth century, but quickly made possible the building of Crystal Palace in London and the great palmhouses elsewhere in Europe and the United States. Because it had previously been so expensive, it had naturally been smart, and nearly all new houses had large blank expanses of plate glass, at least until the Queen Anne revival of the 1880s which brought a return to exaggeratedly small panes and proved that fashion and nostalgia are more powerful factors in architectural change than technological progress. In eighteenth-century architecture look out for the Palladian window shape, with a central arched light and flanking narrow lights, and the gothic windows and glazing which were the predecessors of the large scale gothic revival of the nineteenth century. Fanlights over doors were frequently ornamented with elaborate lead and iron bars, and Dublin is the place to visit to see the greatest concentration of these.

From fanlights we move naturally to doors, the mouth of the house, which may contribute to an expression of genial openness or prim disapproval depending on the way in which it has been treated. Mediaeval doors were built of solid planks and supported on large and elaborate iron hinges. Later, the door became a frame with panels filling up the gaps, which could be varied in proportion and bevelled on the edge to become fielded panels. For the standard Georgian town house, the element of fantasy and display was reserved for the doorway, which was usually given an architectural treatment with columns and a pediment, sometimes elaborated with carving. They are found all over Britain and I saw many good examples in parts of the United States such as Boston. Drawing doors could be a good introduction to the elements of classical architecture.

Until the industrial revolution, there were elements of continuity in most sorts of buildings, particularly in their regional variations. The advent of railway and canal in the nineteenth century brought about a blurring of the old regional differences, and the reduction of much building to a national average of cheap mediocrity. While some regionalism inevitably survived, this is particularly true of the developing industrial areas such as the Midlands in England and the northern parts of the United States. Sensitive Victorians like John Ruskin and William Morris deplored the loss of regional identity in building, and inspired architects at the time to gather their materials locally and revive old crafts where they found them in decay. The result in England was the Arts and Crafts Movement which influenced house building up to the 1930s and may be seen at its best in the garden suburbs and the detached houses built for the prosperous of that period all over the country. Taking the materials and methods of vernacular, or apparently architect-less building, they made new compositions which were often of high artistic quality (like the houses of Edwin Lutyens) without losing the sense of being rooted to a particular locality and its traditions. In the United States architects such as Frank Lloyd Wright worked in much the same way to create the suburbs of cities like Chicago.

Modern architecture aimed at completely different qualities of machine production, universality and infinite extendability, but experience has shown that these buildings are hard to maintain,

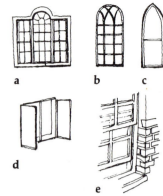

Traditional window types: a the Palladian window, characterized by a central arched light and two others on either side, often decorated with columns and an entablature. b and c represent two stages of the gothic revival: b is typical of the 'Gothick' style of the eighteenth century, while c reflects the development of plate glass in the nineteenth century. d and e: the casement window and sash window.

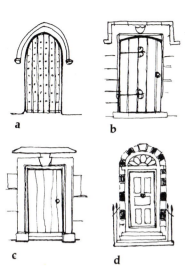

a   b

c   d

Doorways: a medieval arched doorway with a stone 'drip mould', a, and b the sub-medieval doorway developed in the late fourteenth century and commonly used in places such as the Universities of Oxford and Cambridge up to the present century. c might be seen as an eighteenth-century development of this traditional type, while d has all the characteristics of the new Georgian town house: steps, railings, panelled door and elegant fan light.

heat and inhabit, and recent years have seen a welcome return to older methods and crafts, while many people now think it worthwhile to spend time and money giving back life to a decayed old house or cottage, knowing that its mysterious quality and character cannot easily be found in a modern building.

Old houses so often appear to grow in the landscape, either because the landscape has been moulded round them, or because their builders knew what would be a sheltered, well-drained site and preferred these qualities to picture-postcard views seen from the windows of houses which intrude in the landscape in windy, exposed positions.

Buildings which are not houses – churches, temples, monuments and follies – do not of course obey the same rules, and make wonderful subjects for drawing and study. They are often the masterpieces of the high and difficult art of architecture, to which humble building is a necessary prelude. A building of any sort, whether great architecture or not, misses something vital when it is out of sympathy with its surroundings. I often wonder at the way a Moorish palace built in Spain by invaders; using the geometric intricacy of the East, blends so beautifully with the snow-clad mountains surrounding Granada.

A particularly fine eighteenth-century doorway with columns and pediment.

27

Some American Sketches

If you go out looking for interesting architecture, you will always find it, and not always in the places you expect. Once you start looking at the way buildings are put together (and I repeat that the best way of doing this is to draw them) you will soon get an idea of the character of a place you are visiting for the first time.

As an example, I have included in this book a drawing of a house in South Carolina where I stayed when visiting the United States recently for the first time. It looks like the typical American colonial house, and indeed it was built in 1758. In early April, when we were there, it was already hot, and the flowering shrubs and trees festooned with Spanish moss, together with the intensely red earth, made a colourful impression.

The central section of the house was originally a tavern. During the War of Independence the house was occupied by General Cornwallis, followed by General Nathanial Green, whose soldiers burnt the initials CA (Continental Army) into the door with a red-hot poker in 1781. A curious feature of the construction is that the original clapboarding, almost universal in the southern states, was removed in 1821, and the walls were rebuilt in rammed earth, the unusual but practical technique which has already been described. The local red clay was highly suitable for this treatment, and the house forms part of the largest complex of old buildings of this type in the United States.

The walls are built up stage by stage inside shuttering. The clay forms a solid mass which will crack in an earthquake, but not collapse. Inside, wooden studding and laths carry the plaster, leaving an insulated space between. The base coat of this plaster is mixed with rabbit fur and horse hair, similar to the wattle and daub mixture in Britain. The outside is covered with crêpe – a mixture of limestone, clay, sand and blackstrap molasses. Water is added and the resulting slurry is thrown violently against the wall to make it stick, using a besom broom. The present owner has done it himself, and demonstrated the process to me. On top of this is laid a coating of cement pebbledash wash, making the wall impervious to rain. The roof is a very light

The old colonial house, built in 1758, where I stayed in South Carolina. Surrounded by many fine old trees draped with Spanish moss, the mansion house and its outhouses provide a fascinating example of traditional building methods in the United States.

Right Rammed earth construction: this method of building up a clay and earth wall within a timber frame is still in use today.

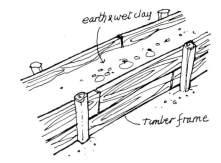

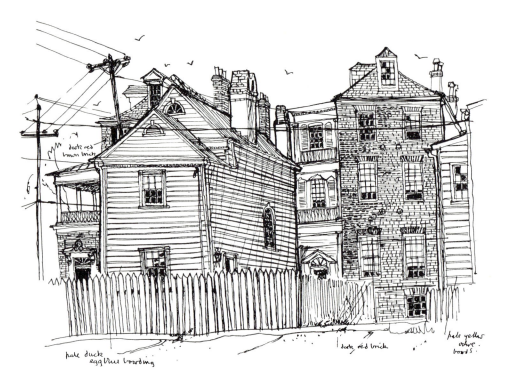

dark red brown brick

pale duck
egg blue bording

dark red brick

pale yellow
ochre.
boords.

No 24 Clifford Street, Charleston, South Carolina. This house stands at right angles to Nos 21 and 22 Archdale Street, both free-standing houses with notable side piazzas; they were restored in 1944 by John D. Muller. Drawn with an Osmiroid fountain pen in 1½ hours; 9" × 6".

construction, now sheathed in copper, its A-frame rafters resting directly on the walls like a hat.

Inside, the old tavern room is thirty-two by eighteen feet, with cellars below, and two original bedrooms above. At the time of the rebuilding wings were added, the chimney moved, and a second-storey porch (or veranda) built over the existing one. The house became the centre of a plantation, with all the additional buildings required by a small self-contained community. All were built of rammed earth: a library, loom house, dry well, doctor's surgery and office, summer kitchen and dairy and, of course, the slave houses. The same

family has lived here continuously, so the house is full of furniture and memorabilia richly evocative of old colonial America.

The materials used for the drawing were much the same as those used for the barn with which this book began; for the first time I experimented with a synthetic brush (Sceptre from Winsor and Newton), which proved excellent and far cheaper than sable. After drawing the outline of the house, portico, pillars and windows, on Cox paper, with a thin pen line, I began to add some colour. For the sky, the area was washed over with clear water first, and prussian blue with a little sepia dropped onto it and allowed to spread. Because of the warmth, it dried quickly, but it was still worth blotting it for texture.

Next came the shape of the tree, and some leaf details with a green made from prussian blue and raw sienna. A blue-green went over the copper roof, and again was quickly blotted. The walls were washed in with a mixture of brown madder alizarin and sepia, carefully painting round the shutters, windows and pillars. If you have not already discovered it, you will quickly learn the importance of keeping a wash moving over the surface of the paper. Once you stop to work on one part, another area may suddenly dry, so that you cannot continue the same colour without an obvious and unsightly break occurring in what should be a continuous surface. The need for speed and concentration makes watercolour the natural medium for recording impressions and moods, as well as accurate detail.

A stronger tone of the same colour served for the steps and pathway and a still darker mixture of sepia, black and blue for the foreground. For the shadows under the eaves more blue was added, and blue again, reflected from the sky, for the shadows in the porch.

The pillars and the balustrade were picked out in white gouache against the yellow Cox-type paper, and thus looked more striking than they might have done if left as blank spaces on white paper. The final stage of the work was to take away the flatness of the white by adding more shadows in blue and sepia, and in addition the pen came into play again for the tree, the windows, and a few shadows of branches which were cast onto the facade. The whole work took two hours.

The plantation house was typical of the wealth of beautiful and interesting building which I found throughout the United States. For me it was a very new discovery, as my knowledge of architecture was previously limited to what I had seen in Europe. In addition, I found that the Americans usually look after their heritage very well, and realize the importance of preserving and rejuvenating whole districts, and not just individual monuments.

This struck me very strongly in Charleston, Edenton and, of course, Williamsburg in Virginia. Leaving New York in April, the change in temperature tells you that you have come south when you arrive in Charleston. The way of life and the way of speaking is much more relaxed and it is perhaps the proverbial Southerner's desire to spend his time sitting on the porch with a mint julep that has enabled the town to preserve so much of its original fabric. It has certainly been helped since 1920 by the Preservation Society of Charleston. In the city centre, flanking the sea, there are more than seventy buildings of the pre-revolutionary period, and

hundreds more date from the early years of independence and the nineteenth century. No intrusions by modern concrete and glass buildings have been allowed here, and only the cars, that perennial hazard to topographical artists, prevented me forgetting about the twentieth century altogether.

The appearance of the old streets is beautiful and the pavements are lined with graceful trees casting moving shadows over the sparkling painted clapboard houses. Some of the streets are paved with pebbles brought over from England as ballast in ships – one of those traditions which one would much rather believe than try to disprove. To im-

This fine Charleston house was originally built for Josiah Smith in brick, despite his wife's preference for a brighter and smarter clapboard house; so much so that after he died a year later, she had it covered with cyprus weatherboarding. Drawn with a Gillott 303 nib and indian ink in two hours; 9" × 7½".

31

prove one's knowledge of the city, there are trips by horse-drawn buses on which the driver explains the history *en route*. Ours was a university undergraduate on vacation.

The abiding impression is of the open verandas, two or more storeys high, running along the sides of the houses, and recalling the days when the street was a spectacle to be enjoyed rather than a dangerous nuisance on which to turn one's back. Along the road facing the sea and Battery, the houses become grander, with two faces of verandas, or piazzas as they are called, from a strange distortion of the Italian word for a town square. They admirably fulfil their function of being cool in the summer evenings, and warm on sunny winter mornings. Furthermore they provide an excellent opportunity for a display of the classical orders of architecture, rising from doric columns on the ground floor to ionic and corinthian on the balconies of the floors above.

In the lesser streets there are houses of brick and stone, rendered and colourwashed, looking very pretty and English. Most of them have shutters, and pantile mansard roofs. There is also a profusion of fine pedimented doorways.

After Charleston, Edenton in North Carolina, a lovely small town on an inlet of Albemarle Sound, extended my experience of the colonial south. The Cupola House was built before 1730, and there are many other eighteenth-century houses with verandas and, to justify my expectations, rocking chairs on them. The houses are beautifully preserved and still lived in.

The journey north took us through some magnificent scenery and dramatic weather. A strong wind whipped up a red dust from the fields, reducing the visibility to twenty or thirty yards in places, the white clapboard houses looming up ahead like paintings by Andrew Wyeth. We approached Virginia through forested countryside, crossing into the state over the James River on a ferry battling against the fierce wind.

Colonial Williamsburg, the object of our journey into Virginia, is a unique place. The original capital of Virginia, it was mostly in ruins in the 1920s when Rockefeller money was brought in to help restore it as a working museum of life in colonial times. Some of the larger buildings were carefully

The Cupola House in Edenton, North Carolina. Built in 1725, this is the oldest house in Edenton and is considered the finest early eighteenth-century house south of Connecticut. Drawn in 45 minutes using a Rotring 2000 isograph pen with an 0.35 nib; 9" × 7".

The Market Hall,
Charleston, South Carolina.
This imposing neo-classical
building is one of the few
built of stone in the area.

Below *The Ewing House, Williamsburg, Virginia. This was built in the late eighteenth century by a Scottish merchant, Ebeneezer Ewing, who used it both as a shop and a home. Note the elegant gambrel roof and the fencing in the foreground, typical to Williamsburg. Drawn with a fibre-tip pen in 30 minutes.*

reconstructed from documents and remaining foundations, and the whole place evokes the taste of the 1920s as well as its original period. The broad central avenue, ninety-nine feet wide, laid out by Governor Francis Nicholson, leads to the imposing Capitol, the original of which was shamefully destroyed by the British in 1781. Apart from the dressing up and make-believe which add to the enjoyment of visiting Williamsburg, it is fascinating to see building work being done according to original methods, with tools like wood planes and adzes.

The contrast with New York could hardly be greater. I was so impressed by the scale and vitality of the city that, like so many other people before, I felt compelled to draw and write my impressions, with words and lines piling on top of each other like skyscrapers. The variety of shapes and styles in the tall buildings was quite unexpected, as was their close concentration in the downtown area. People live in the present, with less respect for the past than elsewhere, but old and new usually seem to combine in the same spirit, from the corinthian temples of the *beaux arts* period skyscrapers, through magnificent examples of art deco like the Chrysler Building, to the bold simplicity and structural skill of buildings like the World Trade Center.

The skyline is famous, but I was unprepared for its actual impact as we drove in from Kennedy Airport in the twilight. It was like a huge, brilliant bracelet lying on its side.

Far left *The Charlton House, West Eden Street, Edenton, North Carolina. The earliest of four eighteenth-century houses built in the area for Jasper Charlton, a lawyer active in Revolutionary politics, and his wife Abigail, the first signatory of the Edenton Tea Party Resolution in 1775. Drawn in 35 minutes with a fibre-tip pen called Le Pen; 5" × 4".*

Left *This charming clapboard house was once, as its large windows might suggest, a shop, named after Robert Davidson, Mayor of Williamsburg in 1738, who ran it as an apothecary's. Drawn with a fine Gillott nib in 40 minutes, 4½" × 3¼".*

The skyscrapers of Manhattan's financial district rising up above Battery Park. Drawn with a 303 Gillott nib and india ink in 1½ hours; 9½" × 7½".

The massive unity of the skyscrapers of Manhattan is impressive and striking and can only be appreciated from a distance. This view of the skyline of Lower Manhattan is taken from Brooklyn. Drawn with a Staedler pen in three-quarters of an hour; 7½" × 2½".

Down in the streets of the city one loses the impressive sight of New York's skyline, and instead discovers a rich variety of architectural styles. This view of Broadway, drawn in 20 minutes while I was having breakfast, is brought to life by the many street and shop signs, as well as the contrasting styles and shapes of lampost, 'phone box and nineteenth-century architecture. Black ink on yellow paper with added white gouache; 7½" × 6".

One of my first paintings was done from the hotel bedroom window as the light faded, and the windows flickered into life in the buildings opposite, like a giant fruit machine.

The weather was still very cold, but it was possible to work out of doors in pen and ink, and the parks offered the opportunity to get far enough away from the tall buildings to allow them to appear as a sort of stage backcloth behind the winter trees. The same effect could be gained by taking a river trip round Manhattan Island. It was a challenge to record the effect of the moving skyline, but New York is a city of challenges, and should incite any artist to do impossible things.

Manhattan from my hotel bedroom window. Gillott 170 and watercolour wash.

Drawn from Hotel Taft
as the night came in.
NEW YORK. 29/3/82.

First Approaches

Travel, interest in buildings, and an appreciation of art: all these are important to the potential artist, but one day you will have to go out and face your subject directly for the first time. To be successful in realizing all that you see and wish to record on paper, you will have to be disciplined in your approach; even practised painters, if their work is not to become routine and dull, must constantly return to essentials and discover new ways of looking.

Rules are made to be broken, but it is just as well to understand why they are there and respect them unless you have good reason not to. In many cases you should follow the rules in the early stages of your work in order to gain the ability to break them successfully later on, when you can develop your style without them.

It hardly needs to be said that a picture translates the three-dimensional real world into a two-dimensional pictorial world, but it is with this that many beginners have the greatest difficulty. It is here that one must develop a painter's eye: that is, an ability to see things in terms of the abstract qualities of pattern and design which lie at the basis of a good picture. In my experience I have found that there are a number of rules or techniques which are basic to developing this ability.

My first rule is to carry a sketchbook wherever I go and use it constantly, sketching buildings and views which appeal to me and seeing how they work on paper. Buildings are easier to understand when they have been drawn, noted and thought out into your sketchbook; it is there to serve as an extension of your mind and eye. A rectangle cut out of the cover of your sketchbook also performs a very useful service: holding it out at arm's length in front of the view which interests you, you will immediately see what that view would look like within the frame of a picture, moving it around in much the same way that a camera view-finder is used. This is perhaps the best way to approach the problem of composition; in choosing a subject to experiment with, avoid anything which is too complicated – a strong skyline and not too much perspective would be a good choice at this stage.

My picture of the National Liberal Club and Whitehall Court seen across the Thames in London provides a good example of this sort of composition, as well as illustrating an important and basic technique in arranging the main features of the view you are painting: I have divided the view up into thirds. In using your cut-out rectangle, it is a good idea to think in terms of such divisions in order to achieve a balanced and effective composition. Here the vertical thirds are marked by the two towers, which fall on the left and right hand divisions, while the horizontal thirds almost co-

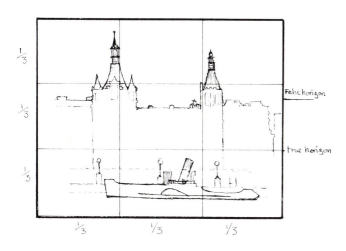

incide with the false and true horizons. Because the two towers are unequal in size they also set up an interesting relationship of balance, which is adjusted by the funnel of the paddle steamer in the foreground. The number three and the triangle have a special importance in art and design, denoting stability and balance; related to this is the ratio of the golden section, dividing a line into two unequal but related parts. This much-used system of proportion, which also occurs throughout the natural world, is best expressed in the diagram below. Here the line has been divided into two parts of 1 and about 1.6 units each. The proportion of 1 to 1.6 is in fact the same as the proportion of 1.6 to the whole line. It is a good idea to bear this system in mind when you tackle composition, if you have not already felt your way instinctively towards it.

Proportion leads naturally to balance, the next

Below left *The golden rectangle, the system of proportion from which the thirds division in the* Whitehall Court picture is *ultimately derived.*
Below right *Balance: showing how the larger* tower, just off-centre, is *balanced by the smaller one at the far left of the composition.*

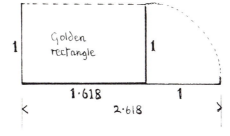

The Houses of Parliament from the South Bank, pen and watercolour, 16" × 6", drawn in 2 hours as the sun set in the background. The composition here is fairly loose, built up around the central emphasis of the tower of Big Ben. Otherwise colour is used to create a sense of balance – the distinctive buildings at either end of the picture prevent it from melting away into nothing, while the red London buses crossing Westminster Bridge add a contrasting note to the mass of the Parliament buildings beyond.

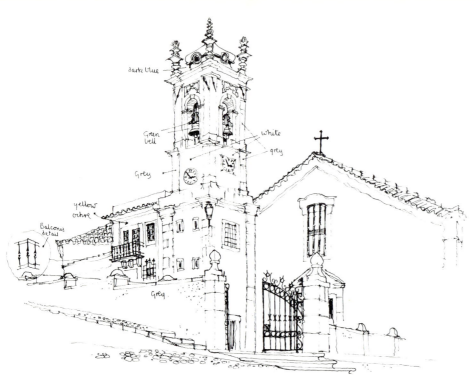

Labels on the drawing:
dark blue
Green bell
white
grey
Grey
yellow ochre
Balcony detail
Grey

Church at Sesimbra, near Lisbon, Portugal. 11" × 8½", drawn in 50 minutes with a Faber-Castell fine pen.

Below, *this diagram shows the two-point perspective system used in drawing the church.*

vanishing point eye level vanishing point

important factor in composition. The simplest way of explaining balance is by the analogy of a see-saw on a pivot: to achieve a central emphasis when the main elements in your picture are of an unequal weight, they should be arranged around the centre in such a way that a sense of balance is maintained – in much the same way that two unequal weights on a see-saw might be placed. This is the basis of the Whitehall Court picture, where the larger tower left-of-centre is balanced by the smaller one at the right hand end of the picture.

In considering balance one should also take into account other factors such as colour, texture and shading. When you look at things, think of them as hard, soft, rough, smooth, shiny, matt, warm or cool in colour, jagged or regular in outline, and see how these qualities set up balances within a composition. Think also of the qualities of different colours – as Constable discovered, a speck of scarlet will set off a field of green and bring it to life. The reason why many landscape painters enjoy dark skies is because they set off the other colours in the picture, as in thundery weather. Dawn and dusk are favourite times for painters, not only for their romantic associations, but because the nearly horizontal light brings out the richness of colours which is lost in the glare of mid-day. These secondary lights are cut out in reflection, so try looking sometimes in a mirror at the view you are painting, or in the reflection of a plate glass window.

These considerations are universal to all paintings; in the specialized branch of architectural painting, good drawing is essential, as here line is perhaps even more important than the questions of mass and colour which have already been discussed. The balance of these elements in any particular style is up to the individual artist to decide, and you must determine, for each new subject, how much drawing is required – whether the detail helps you to see and understand or, as is sometimes the case, gets in the way of the essential forms. Whatever your decision, a knowledge of the working of perspective is fundamental to the artist's ability to use line.

Do not let perspective take you over as a painter, as can easily happen; its most important use is to enable you to look at objects analytically and understand how they work in space. The best way to begin is to return to the cut-out frame in the cover of your sketchbook. Looking through it at a view, concentrate on how the lines of the major objects you can see move up and down or from side to side, ignoring for the moment whether or not these objects recede in depth. Treat the view you can see through the frame you are holding up as being two-dimensional, on a flat plane: the lines which mark the edge of buildings do not recede in depth, they just run at an angle away from the vertical or horizontal. These angles are then transcribed to another flat plane – your drawing pad. It was by such simple methods that the great intellectual painters of the Renaissance established the rules of perspective which permanently changed the art of the western world.

The basis of perspective is the vanishing point. All parallel lines which recede from the picture plane will appear to converge on this point, which may or may not be located within the frame of your picture, depending on your position in relation to the object in perspective. My sketch of the little church at Sesimbra in Portugal (*opposite*) provides a simple example of two-point perspective, in

An abandoned Cotton Gin near Camden, South Carolina, drawn with Finepoint felt pens, sizes 0.2 and 0.4. 8½" × 5", one hour.

This diagram shows the simple one-point perspective on which the drawing of the Cotton Gin is based.

vanishing point

eye level

43

Ray Evans
House by the Itchen

Left *A house by the River Itchen, near Winchester. The white bridge in the foreground shows the sort of effect which can be achieved by masking with Frisk film.*

A watercolour sketch of a street in Rovinj, Yugoslavia; 12″ × 9″.

which there are two vanishing points. The first object is to establish the horizon line, which is at the eye-level of the artist. Here it runs near the bottom of the page, at about the height of the lowest steps leading to the church. The two vanishing points are discovered by following the horizontal lines of the church tower until they meet with the horizon line. All other parts of the church building, or other buildings in alignment with it, will be governed by these two points; despite the road rising at the left, the top of the wall follows the same system of perspective, which can easily be understood and mastered.

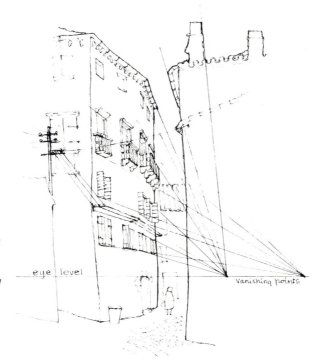

This diagram shows how there are a number of different vanishing points along the length of the eye level, corresponding with the changing angles on the facade of the building on the left. In practice it is probably easier to tackle a subject like this without relying on accurate vanishing points; a grid would be more helpful.

Some subjects will have many different vanishing points, and to develop your skill in tackling these you might practise projecting simple rectilinear forms on paper. You will probably not want to work this way in the field, but it is a good thing to have an idea where the vanishing point for each plane ought to be. To get the angle of a line running sharply away, it is helpful to hold up a pen or pencil on the line, see what angle it makes with the vertical, and bring it down immediately onto the paper, looking up again to check. If in doubt, put a few dots where you think the line ought to go, check again with your pencil in the air, and see if it is right. The watercolour sketch of Rovinj (page 45) is a good example of multiple-point perspective: as the street drops away to the right and the buildings curve round, there are few planes which are either parallel or at right angles to each other, with the result that there are a number of different vanishing points on the horizon line.

A traditional method of drawing complex subjects is by means of a glass screen with a grid on it. A similar grid is drawn on the paper or canvas, where the scene is recreated square by square; although this method may sound mechanical it is useful and can lead to sketches which are accurate and yet retain a fresh and spontaneous feel. Here it is illustrated by a grid and sketch for La Grande Rue in Dieppe. There is one central vanishing point for the buildings on the left and right in the foreground. However, as the buildings in the background curve to the right, their vanishing points also move along the horizon line to the right. Where there are so many vanishing points within one scene a grid will make the task of drawing it far easier, even allowing you, if you prefer, to

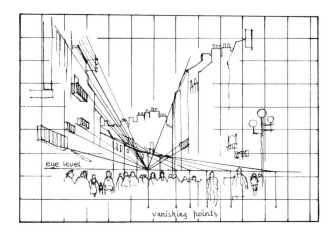

eye level

vanishing points

ignore perspective altogether and judge each angle of window, roof or door in each of the grid squares, using the lines of the grid to make sure that all these parts are in correct relation to each other.

In first tackling the problems of perspective it is far easier to draw your subjects sight size; by this method you work out the scale of the buildings you are painting by holding your pencil at arm's length and using your thumb on the side of the pencil to measure off the proportions of your subject. These measurements are then transferred directly to your drawing. The technique is particularly useful when it comes to the difficult business of drawing curved forms in perspective. Circular objects seen in perspective – cartwheels, arches, round ponds, and so on – will always appear as regular ovals. Using your pencil to measure off the long and short axes of the oval, sketch these in lightly on your drawing and then add the circumference of the shape around them. This same method should be used in drawing an

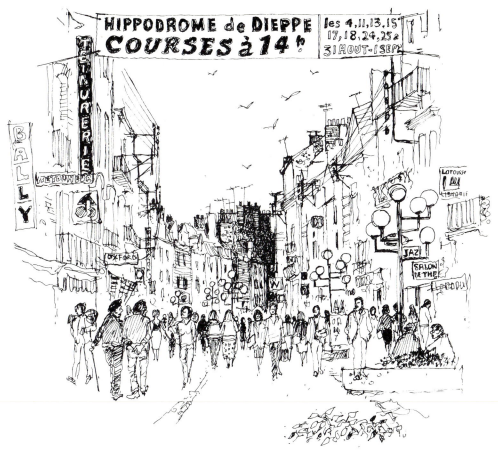

La Grande Rue, Dieppe, drawn in about 30 minutes. The diagram illustrates how a grid can be used together with an eyel level line and vanishing point in order to get the right angles of the buildings on your drawing. As the buildings in the background curve to the right a number of new vanishing points appear on the eye level line, as in the sketch of the Rovinj street.

arch, although only the top half of the oval shape appears in reality. Remember that the arch will appear to slope forwards toward the viewer, because the line from which the arch springs cuts through the oval at an angle.

You will find that the many problems posed by perspective become much easier to solve when you have a good background knowledge of building construction and design. This is particularly true in the case of classical architecture, where questions of proportion and balance are essential to the character of a building. A trained eye will quickly pick out both the basic structure and subtle details of a building – for instance the use of entasis, the slight widening of the top half of columns which was developed by the classical architects in order to counter the appearance of narrowing which is caused by perspective. In all this it is important to retain a sense of scale, and the best way of doing this is by introducing some feature which can act as a gauge. For instance, in the painting of Whitehall Court discussed earlier, the figures on the boat establish its size, while the traffic moving on the Embankment beyond allows one to judge the scale of Whitehall Court itself. With composition, balance and perspective, scale can be used to discipline one's method of looking at and drawing architecture, making one's work clearer and more easily intelligible.

These, then, are the basic guidelines to be borne in mind when you first approach your subject; they should be understood and mastered, but they should not become an overriding concern in one's work. Very often in my own painting they are not immediately apparent, as for instance in *Farm near Llansawel, Wales*, which represents a favourite style

of picture: hardly any obvious perspective and a central vanishing point around which the composition appears, at first sight, to be very loosely arranged. Although a rather stark subject, I was immediately attracted by the abstract qualities of the dark farmhouse with its regular window openings, seeming to sit almost on top of the white iron gate flanked on each side by red brick posts.

These abstract qualities give the final composition its sense of structure; at the centre of the picture there is a triangular frame, the points of which are provided by the farmhouse and the two gateposts. This shape is repeated within the gate itself,

Farm near Llansawel, Wales, opposite. *This watercolour (10" × 7") was used for the Abbey National 1983 Calendar.*

A line drawing of the farm near Llansawel. Perspective is not a very important element in this composition; instead features such as the dark farmhouse, the bright red tractor and the red gateposts provide the basic structure of the picture.

red tractor
slates/gate roof
house dark ochre colours
red brick pillars.

white gate

49

the two strengthening bars pointing directly at the red tractor which happened to be placed in the centre as the strongest note of colour. The gable end of the barn on the left provides another subsidiary triangle, and is balanced by a lower barn on the right. Thus the structure within the composition was discovered in the view itself, rather than being imposed on it; there is a natural orderliness about a group of buildings like this which easily translates itself into painting. The eye-level is exactly half way up the picture, something which is academically incorrect, but I think the strength of the triangular form overrides this fault, which would be more serious in a seascape or flat landscape.

The only work done on the spot was a line drawing, but I also took a colour slide for use when reconstructing the scene in the studio. The painting was done on a rough surface Saunders watercolour board. After careful drawing of the main features, the sky was painted in prussian blue with a touch of black, not too much lest the colour become opaque and dirty. It had been a wild April day, and the best way of getting the effect of a moving sky was to wash out the colour under the tap before it was quite dry.

Next came the fields and hills, again mainly in blue, but with some raw sienna, then the house and tractor, and the ground behind the white gate.

It might have been better to get a sharp edge on the gate by masking it out and washing all over the background, but in fact I left the bars of the gate as white paper. Then I followed the barn roofs and wall tops. For the gateposts, it was important to paint each brick individually, as their variations in colour had attracted me to the subject in the first place, echoing the red of the tractor. They also acted as a foil to the farm windows. The slate roof and the window panes were very dark, and I blotted the roof to give it texture.

At this point the foreground needed strengthening, so it was washed over in sepia ink, and after only a few seconds (because it is a waterproof ink) it went under the tap again. As in other works, a little white gouache was useful at this stage for bringing up highlights, and for strengthening the white gate. It is difficult to make this paint runny enough to work easily without losing its covering power, so I used it thickly and blotted off the surface of it. Some penwork at the end sharpened up the details where necessary.

Although I used several different media, the general effect was one of watery transparency. The picture was mounted in grey with a white slip and two white lines, within a dull silver frame with two black lines. The red underpainting of the frame showed through, and contributed to the success of the final effect.

Equipment and Materials

The materials which you use and buy must be divided into those which can be carried and those that will only work in the studio, or if travelling directly to a subject by car. It is just as well to keep both categories down to the practical minimum, and not be attracted by too many gadgets which may be distracting you from the proper business of looking and painting. You will make your own discoveries and establish your preferences, but here for what it is worth is my choice of materials:

Pencils   Several grades from 4B to F, and perhaps multiples of softer ones if you use them often. You can then sharpen a batch of them before starting work and save time. It is best to sharpen with a knife blade for a longer point. Coloured pencils, carbon and conté pencils can be useful as pocket equipment, or you might, like several recent artists, specialize in coloured crayon work.

Pens   Steel nibs made by Gillots and other manu-facturers; these are inexpensive and it is worth in-

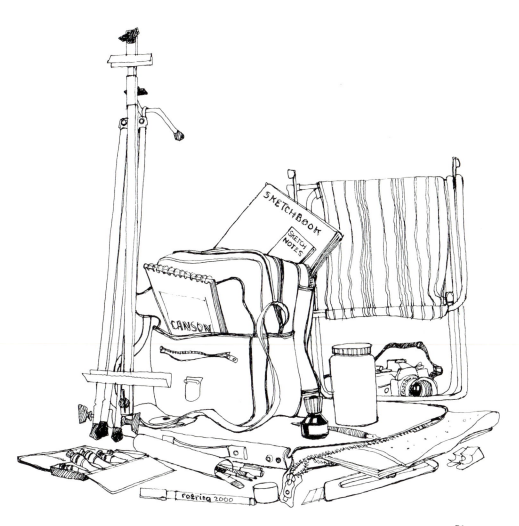

Outdoor equipment: a carrying bag with large side pockets is the basic essential. Into this should go the water jar, watercolour box, tube for holding brushes and pencils, an india ink pen with a bottle of india ink, wind clips and a knife. A folding stool and light easel complete the kit.

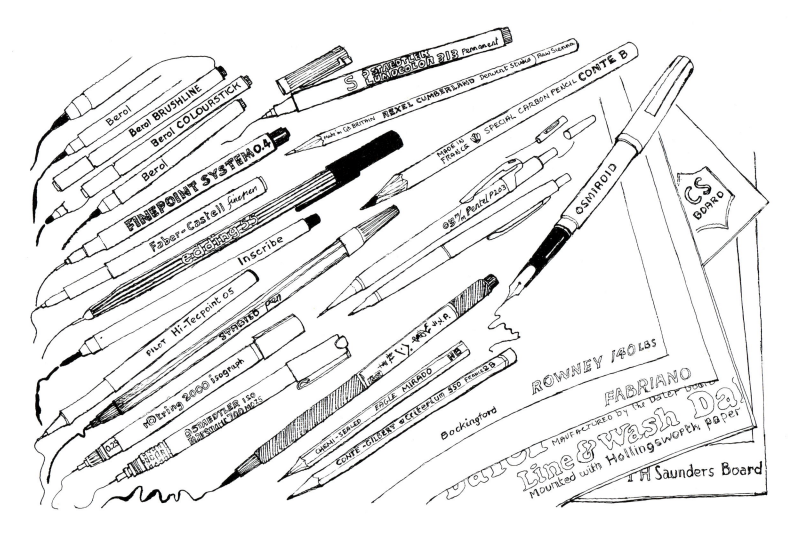

A range of the fibre pens, felt pens, fountain pens and pencils commonly available, *shown together with papers and boards suited to drawing and watercolour work.*

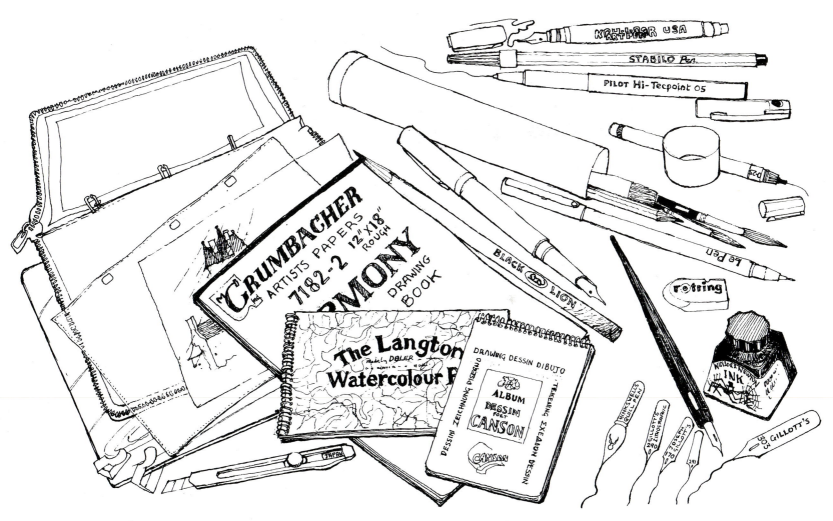

A portfolio is essential for carrying drawings; ideally it should be equipped with plastic holders which are useful for display and protection. Shown with it are a pen and brush holder, with a range of pens: Koh-i-Nor art pen, Stabilo felt tip, Pilot, Rotring and Le Pen (the last three all suited to line drawing). At the bottom is a dip pen and a range of Gillott nibs. Finally, two small but essential items – a knife and wind clips.

53

vesting in plenty of them and finding which ones suit you. Don't omit to try the broader ones.

Rotring, Staedler, Rapidograph and other stylographic pens are invaluable. They take Indian (waterproof) ink without clogging; draw with ease in any direction and encourage decisiveness and linear clarity. They do, however, need to be cleaned often.

Felt and fibre pens are usually water soluble and no good with watercolour, unless you want a deliberately blurred effect. They give even more freedom of movement than stylographic pens and are now available in very fine points. At the other end of the scale there are pens with chinese brush hairs for painterly effects.

Brushes For watercolour work these must be soft but firm. The traditional hair for brushes is sable, which has always been very expensive, but it is worth getting the best grade when buying the smaller brushes. For these, each hair is individually selected for length and curved inwards towards a point. Try out the brush in water in the shop and make sure that all the hairs are in place. Look after the brush well, washing it out after use, and occasionally in soap in the palm of the hand to get accumulated paint out of the depths. Well treated, a brush lasts for many years.

Because sables are so well made, a size like No. 6 will both carry a lot of paint and have a fine enough point for most detailed work. One smaller brush is also an advantage, but be sure also to get at least one larger one. Large flat brushes are an economy and enable one to work closely up to a line.

On no account use inferior cheap brushes; your painting time is too valuable to be spent in coping with their manifold inadequacies. On the other hand, the new synthetic sable brushes, while occasionally lacking the delicacy of the real thing, are an acceptable and much cheaper substitute.

When you travel keep your brushes in a sealed, cylindrical container and attach them to a slightly longer rod inside with a rubber band to prevent the tips getting knocked about. For the studio various brush holders and washers are available at a reasonable price.

Paint Watercolours are the most portable form of paint, and provide most of the effects needed for a graphic, linear style of architectural painting, although there are many other ways of using them. The paint consists of pigment bound in water-soluble gum arabic. In *tubes*, the gum is slightly diluted, in *pans* the pigment is more concentrated. It is perhaps best to combine the two types, using tubes for the colours you use most frequently in quantity, or for colours like yellows and bright reds which easily get dirty in the pan. A box of eight whole pans will give you enough colours for most purposes, with some of the rarer ones in half pans. Choose your own colours, and never buy a pre-fitted box. The initial outlay is great, but the colour is strong and will last for a long time. A few tubes will fit into the central space in the box meant for brushes (but always too short). Others can be carried in a separate tin, and squeezed out into the mixing wells in the lid of the box as required.

Work out your own system for water – there are specially made water bottles with a dipper to hook onto the edge of the box, but a good method is to use a flat-bottomed white plastic wash-saucer rest-

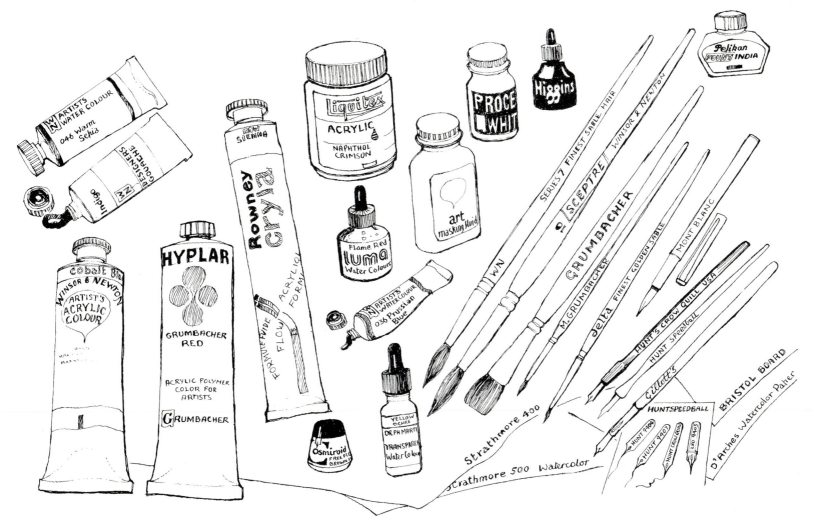

Watercolour paints are probably most easily carried around in tubes, as shown above, together with acrylic paints. Of the brushes shown the Winsor and Newton Series 7 is perhaps the most commonly used size, while the larger sizes, particularly the Grumbacher, are ideal for applying washes. A range of brushes should also include the ones, as shown, for detailed work, while the dip pens illustrated work well with other mediums, as well as being versatile and easy to use.

55

A terrace of houses in Bradford, Yorkshire (9½" × 6½"). Drawn, in 1½ hours, with B, 2B and 4B Rowney Victoria pencils, the different hardnesses of pencil giving a varied effect over the whole drawing.

ing on the flat inner flap of the box, and renew the water when you see it getting dirty. You can also use these saucers for mixing special washes for a large area like the sky. A box such as this is large enough for sketching and studio work, but if you like to travel light, there are miniature sketcher's boxes, although a few tubes of paint in an old tobacco tin will do nearly as well.

Choice of colours   always buy the best artist's quality which are more economic in the long run. Always buy colours which are tested for permanency, usually marked 'selected list', as there are others which fade rapidly in the light. For the choice of pigments themselves, find your own way, but here are some personal preferences:

Reds: scarlet lake, winsor red, carmine, rose madder (delicate pink), and chrome orange;

Blues: prussian blue, ultramarine, antwerp blue, indigo (valuable for mixing);

Browns: brown madder alizarin, burnt sienna, warm sepia;

Purples: winsor violet;

Greens: (these are often best mixed, or at least modified) olive green, winsor green, viridian;

Blacks and Greys: lamp or ivory black, charcoal grey, payne's grey and neutral tint – all useful for bluish shadows;

Yellows: new gamboge, indian yellow, raw sienna, chinese white.

Paper The choice is still wide, although papers go rapidly in and out of production. The main difference is between *hand-made* and *mould-made* and between *rag* and *pulp*. Rag paper is an affordable luxury as it receives the paint gratefully, and is

very strong, as well as being chemically nearly acid-free and so theoretically eternal. It is usually made in three surfaces – rough, not (i.e. not pressed, also described as cold or medium pressed), and hot pressed (smooth). The first two will probably be the most useful. There are also light laid papers like Ingrès, which like the Canson-Montgolfier Mi-Teintes come in a wide range of colours. Other popular coloured papers come in indigo and rough pale yellow, together with various re-creations of the David Cox paper, which was originally wrapping paper discovered

Also in Bradford, this drawing (9½″ × 6½″) on cartridge paper took 35 minutes, using a Pilot Hi-Techpoint 05 pen. These brick and slate buildings are typical of the working class housing of the nineteenth century in this area.

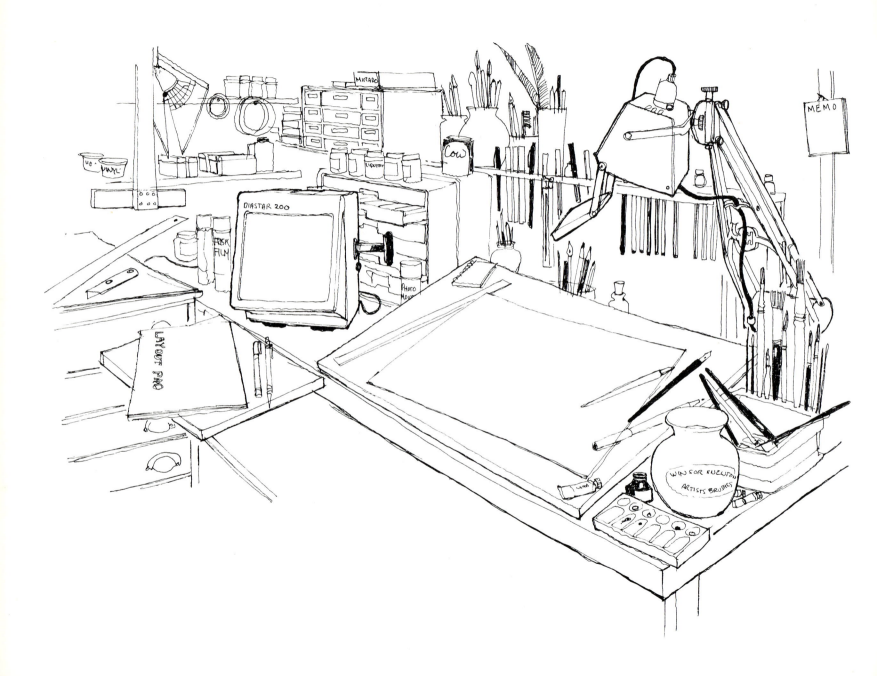

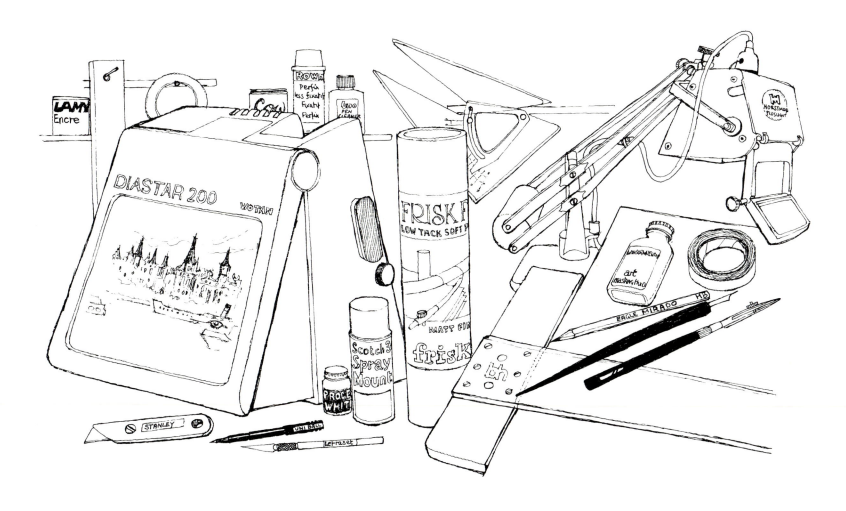

A studio need not be very large, and by clearing my work bench, **left**, I can easily handle even the larger panoramic watercolours I paint. A north-east facing window above the work bench gives a good, uniform light, while shelves keep equipment and reference books within easy reach. The plan chest should also be easily accessible.

A projector such as the Diastar shown above provides the best method for viewing slides. Other equipment illustrated includes a tee square (in transparent plastic) and behind the lamp, an adjustable set square.

The Temple of Octavius in Rome, drawn with pen, wash and gouache on a coloured paper.

by this nineteenth-century watercolourist. For sketching in pen or pencil without much colour wash, cartridge, smooth board or even thin bank paper are very useful. Most papers come in several different weights, usually measured in lbs. for a ream of 500 sheets, so that 140 lbs. is heavy, 50 lbs. a very light paper. The international metric standard based on grams per square metre (gsm) is now replacing this. The watermark on the paper may give the weight and the maker's name.

Depending on the wetness of your technique, you may like to stretch the lighter papers onto a board by wetting them and sticking down the edges with a brown gum strip.

Watercolour paper usually comes in sizes of about thirty by twenty-two inches and should be halved or quartered according to your needs. It is a good recommendation for beginners to work mainly on half this size, as the large scale helps to establish confidence and a sense of design, and prevents fussing and niggling. It is much easier to reduce to a smaller size afterwards, if desired, than to move up to a larger size when you are not used to it.

Sketchbooks can be brought ready made in a variety of shapes and sizes, and types of paper. Whether you use these or loose sheets of paper in a zip portfolio is a matter of personal preference depending on how you like to organize your work. I like to have sketchbooks made up with paper of my choice by a local bookbinder and usually start a new one for each trip. Made like this, they open flat with ease and enable you to work across the join in two pages. However there are also many excellent ready-made sketchbooks on the market to choose from.

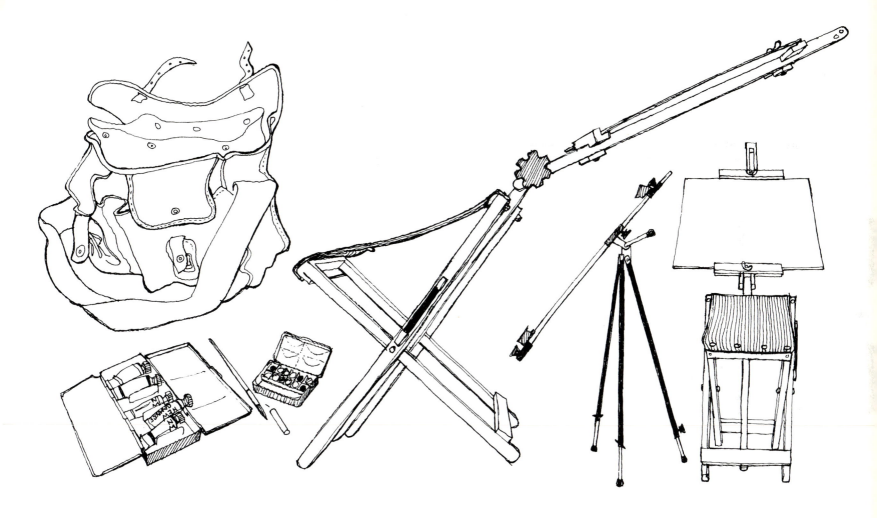

A fishing bag, as shown above, is large and can easily accommodate the variety of equipment, from bars of chocolate upwards, which one is ever likely to need outdoors. The 'sit and sketch' easel and seat, made by Amelia Anson Associates, is very light and handy. Beside it are the light easel, shown erected, and a watercolour box with tubes together with a mixing box.

Amateurs with little studio time available may prefer to work mainly on individual sheets, stretched or not, and do most of the painting on the site. My preference is for sketchbooks, with paintings and drawings worked up to whatever degree the subject demands and the circumstances permit. The books make attractive objects, and the new sketchbook, at the beginning of a holiday or tour, is full of exciting unfulfilled possibilities.

Easels, stools etc Compactness and comfort are often at odds. The best stool has a light aluminium frame, and a strong seat of plastic fibre. Other seats have been known to give one appalling pins and needles or land one in the gutter when surrounded by curious foreign children. The traditional tripod seat with a triangular leather top is more comfortable, but heavy and awkward to carry. Easels are generally dispensible out of doors, unless you like

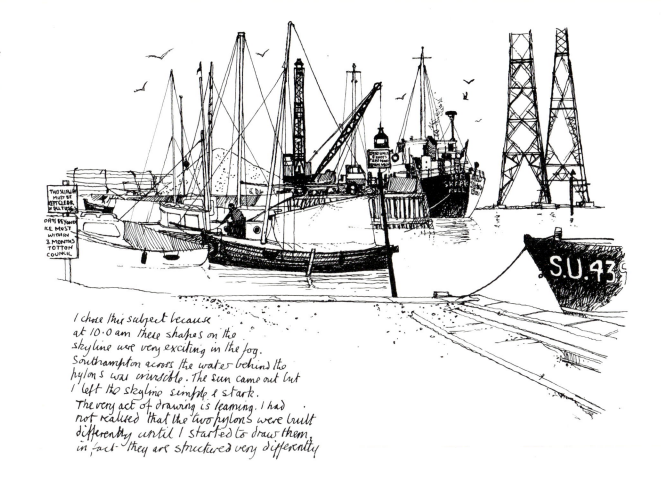

Eling Creek, Southampton, drawn in two hours on a foggy February morning with a Gillott 170 nib and india ink, finishing it off with a fountain pen. The drawing, on smooth cartridge paper, measures 9½" × 6".

I chose this subject because at 10.0 am these shapes on the skyline were very exciting in the fog. Southampton across the water behind the pylons was invisible. The sun came out but I left the skyline simple & stark.
The very act of drawing is learning. I had not realised that the two pylons were built differently until I started to draw them, in fact they are structured very differently

to have your painting upright in the same plane as the subject; in this case there are many good light easels on the market. Otherwise a board or portfolio on the knees is just as good. At home an angled board on a bench or table is quite adequate.

Carrying bag A fishing bag with a waterproof lining is excellent. A canvas bag with little leather straps made for gamekeepers to carry pheasant feed is beautifully made and very strong, and is also big enough to take a portfolio and stool.

Field and Studio Work

There are many motives for drawing buildings; the pleasure of the buildings themselves, the enjoyment of going out sketching on a fine day in summer, the desire to exhibit work as an amateur, and for a few lucky people like me, the fact that it is one's livelihood.

All these motives overlap to some degree, but it depends on which one predominates in choosing which is the best method of work to adopt. If you wish your work to have that permanent quality which makes it worth framing and hanging on a wall, you will take some pride in it, and want it to look as good as possible in itself, as well as being a truthful record of something seen. Working out of doors is the best way of developing your skills – you are subject to a variety of annoyances, but the capacity to soldier on will probably have a favourable effect on your work. Faced with these various distractions – for instance by occasional supercilious adults who give you irrelevant advice and information – you may begin to wonder whether it would be easier to stay at home and do all your work in the studio.

Outdoors you are also at the mercy of non-human factors – changing light, uncertain weather, and in towns, the noise and congestion of traffic. My watercolour and pen drawing of the Porte D'Auteuil is a typical product of such a situation, painted on a bright showery day from a public roadside bench, contending with the worst of the Paris rush hour. I knew that it was probably not a suitable sketch for a painting but sometimes I draw for no other reason except that I love to.

Speed was of the essence, and I handled the white elements, such as the windows and lettering on the large advertisement, by painting around them and leaving them as blank paper. The building was painted in four of my favourite colours, alizarin brown madder, prussian blue, raw sienna and warm sepia. I wanted to catch the effect of the quick changes of light and shade from the clouds and flashes of sunlight, darkening the top of the building against the sky and blotting as I drew in order to speed up the process. Finally, I pulled the whole composition together with pen and Indian ink, putting in a few highlights with gouache. This is a favourite method when using colour and this sort of quick drawing fills many sketchbook pages.

The sketch of Rovinj, in Istria, Yugoslavia, (pages 72–3) is a similar sort of outdoor piece of work, although it was drawn in more relaxed circumstances, from outside a cafe while drinking a coffee. Again I worked quickly with a limited range of colours, and again I was aiming at catching the atmosphere of movement and bustle on the crowded waterfront. It is a good idea to concentrate

Sketching in Paris.
Right *the Porte D'Auteuil, 6¼" × 8", drawn in watercolour and a dip pen and india ink for the outlines.*
Far right *the Palais Royale, a quick, 25 minute watercolour sketch measuring 7" × 3½".*

watercolour
drip her side.

Palais
Royale
1x8/9/74

Winchester Cathedral, east front. A quick watercolour sketch using a No 4 brush on water-colour paper, with warm sepia, brown madder alizarin, raw sienna, prussian blue and a little black. Pen line was added with a 170 Gillott nib. Measuring 7″ × 5½″, it took about 40 minutes.

The same view of the Cathedral, right after scaffolding had been erected for restoration work. Measuring 14″ × 10″, this version, more carefully finished and intended for publication, took 2 hours. A Gillott 303 nib was used on watercolour board. Although meticulous, the drawing retains a sense of freedom, especially in the treatment of the bare trees in the foreground.

on figures either approaching you or walking away from you, as these will remain in your view for longest; in this case I was lucky as the group of fishermen on the right seemed to remain static for quite some time.

As in the Parisian sketch, I painted the scene broadly leaving large areas of white, blotting as I went and working quickly but in a relaxed way, adding a little colour where necessary and not caring too much about accuracy. I was quite pleased with the result and certainly enjoyed drawing it.

In spite of all the drawbacks to working outdoors, it can be very stimulating, and you can quickly make friends with people even in a country where you do not speak the language. Working on site is also of primary importance as it is only by drawing and observing buildings that knowledge, skill and ideas can be developed. To start with you may find, like William Blake, that 'Nature puts you out' and that there is too much to look at, but it is best to develop your own personal stylizations of the things you see in front of the real objects, instead of copying them from other artists. Only by sitting in front of a subject do you begin to realize the changing qualities of different lights and skies, and begin to notice all sorts of things which may not have been evident at first glance. A considerable mental effort of concentration is required, but like all effort, it is ultimately rewarded, and you will find that the most difficult subjects often lead you forward into new directions in your work. Your personal style will begin to form without any conscious effort, and then you will be ready for the alternative and supplementary process of working in the studio.

Perhaps the greatest challenge to the beginner is

The Medieval House: two ancient cottages at South Harting in West Sussex. Although this picture is highly finished, it was painted outdoors, in 2 hours, from my car. Commissioned for the 1983 Abbey National Calendar.

choosing the right view and selecting the elements which are essential to producing a finished painting later on. Often one must use a number of sketches to produce a painting which combines features of all of them. For instance my Amsterdam street scene (pages 116–7) was painted from sketches (page 131) which were made from angles. Very often it is not possible to sketch the particular view you want because of traffic, for instance, and in this situation a camera can be useful. I rarely work from photographs alone but on occasion they are essential.

The Mediaeval House opposite provides an example of a sketch which had to have a high degree of finish, as it was part of a commission for thirteen views for a calendar. Altogether I took two hours over the sketch, painting from my car after finding the best viewpoint available. To begin with I made a small pen sketch in order to get the feel of the house, which looked like a prehistoric monster with its great head of thatch. The thatch was beautifully done and must have excellent insulation properties.

As the subject was quite complicated I began with a B pencil, lightly touching in all the main features instead of painting it broadly. Then I painted the roof, washing in the large mass of thatch and letting it dry slightly. I filled it in with warm sepia and the merest touch of prussian blue, blotting a little to give texture to the reeds. I carried on down with the same colour over the timber, again blotting with the effect of giving it an antique look. With the same brush I painted in the bits of rendering on the wall with raw sienna.

The brickwork was painted carefully with a finer brush, varying a mixture of burnt sienna, brown

Bridge over the River Conwy at Llanrwst in Wales. Designed in 1636 by Inigo Jones, this attractive three arched bridge was sketched hurriedly in 45 minutes, any further work on it prevented by the heavy raindrops which began to fall from the dark and overcast sky. I used a dip pen with a Gillott 170 nib and black and brown india ink; the dark sky was filled in with a blue-black wash. Drawn on thin cartridge paper measuring 11" × 6".

The Three Brewers Pub in Islington, London opposite, left. In this quick 40 minute sketch I used two Rotring pens, one with brown and the other with black ink.

Colour notes are useful for more detailed work in the studio (6" × 7").

Within the drawings, handwritten colour notes:
grey purple · light chocolate brown · dark yellow bricks · red Skol · cream · white letter · yellow · brown lettery · chocolate brown

Bill Bentley's Wine Bar in London and Laurence Oxley's Bookshop in New Alresford (above right and *right) are both preliminary studies for watercolours, drawn with Rotring pens in black and brown ink. They* *both took about 40 minutes, the former measuring 11" × 8" and the latter 8" × 9".*

madder alizarin, raw sienna, warm gamboge and a little black, using blotting paper in order to give the surface variety and texture. Then the background of trees were washed in with a mixture of prussian blue, a little black and a touch of raw sienna; the grass in the foreground with a mixture of new gamboge and raw sienna, and the road grey, leaving white lines for relief.

Finally I filled in the shadows on the roof and wall with a mixture of prussian blue and black, washing out some of this colour with a large brush and blotting it when the picture was nearly dry. The window panes were darkened, varying the shades to give the whole a sparkle. I picked out details with pen and ink, concentrating on the focal point of the picture at the centre of the building, and flicked in a few rooks which were flying about the house. The sky I left quite blank in order to contrast with the bulk of the building.

This is a very complete sketch, but it retains a vitality and sense of immediacy which is typical of sketching, so much so that even a third party can recognize the difference between work in the field and studio work quite easily. It is at this point, when one has attained a confidence and facility outdoors, that one should face the different problems of working indoors. You will need somewhere to work at home, according to the scale of your work and the media you use. For modest size watercolours, the dining room table is usually perfectly adequate, or, better still, a table where the equipment can stay in place, and there is enough light. North light has always been ideal, but you seldom get it out of doors where sunlight alternates with shadow, so do not worry unduly if you fail to get it within.

72

The waterfront at Rovinj, Yugoslavia, drawn from outside a cafe. In order to capture the atmosphere with a fairly quick outdoor sketch the scene was painted broadly, using washes in a limited range of colours and adding structural details, and the distinctive skyline of television aerials, in pen.

*Praca da Figuera, Lisbon,
left drawn in 45 minutes
from a cafe terrace with a
Pilot fibre tipped fine pen
(11½" × 8¼"). There was
a lot of movement, and the
figures drawn in greatest
detail are those which were
walking towards me.*

*Mosteiro dos Jeronimos,
Belem, Portugal (11½" ×
8"). Drawn with a fine felt
tip pen, this sketch took
about 45 minutes.*

The Prospect of Whitby, an old inn on the Thames in Wapping, London. Painted on rough Saunders watercolour board measuring 11″ × 6″. I used a limited palette of the following Winsor and Newton artist's watercolours: prussian blue, raw sienna, scarlet lake, olive green, and warm sepia. Brushes used included various sizes of Winsor and Newton's Sceptre series 606 square ended brushes; numbers 10, 6, 2 and 1 of series 101 brushes; and a 1″ and ½″ house painter's brush.

The first stage was a line drawing (top left) with a conté grade B pencil. The sky was then washed with a number 10 brush, using cleaned water; this made it easier to apply the colour wash of prussian blue, raw sienna, and a little olive green. Before this was completely dry I washed it out with the 1″ brush, causing some of the colour to come out and lighten areas of the sky, giving texture to the whole; blotting added to this effect.

The roofs were painted with a number 6 brush in blue and warm sepia, and then blotted. A mixture of olive green, raw sienna and warm sepia was used to build up the timbers on the quayside and the quayside itself (leaving the figure '5' white). The hull, masts and sails of the barge were then painted with a number 6 brush using red, warm sepia and raw sienna with blue and olive green on the upper part of the hull. A number 1 brush was used for the details on the boat and the inn, the lettering on the front of it being left white.

At this stage (bottom right) the white wall of the inn was stained with raw sienna. The detailed work was continued with a fine pen and a number 1 brush, darkening the roofs and window panes and strengthening such details as the rigging, seagulls and figures and deepening the shadows of the quayside. At this final stage, in order to prevent the contrasts being too sharp, a wash of prussian blue with a little warm sepia was used on the inn and quayside, washing out and blotting before it was dry.

In the studio you can experiment in a concentrated and undisturbed way with the varied material brought in from outside. You must develop different skills and techniques, trying out different effects of light and shade, varying composition and viewpoint, and, if necessary, taking advantage of the toughness of stretched watercolour paper or board and putting the whole thing under a tap and washing it out in order to obtain interesting textures. At the end of the day you must aim to expand your methods and intensify the effect of your work; this, quite simply, is how Turner arrived at the wonderful work of his later period, usually beginning from little more than pencil sketches.

Studio work is likely to be for special commissions, as much as for uninhibited experiments. A working method is useful, and the traditional technique of squaring up a sketch and enlarging it is

Milnathort, near Loch Leven (10½" × 5½"). Although the keep on the left is now a ruin, the right hand side of this Scottish castle is still inhabited.

This charming little church at Somborne was drawn with a Rotring 0.25 nib on thin watercolour paper. Although a sketch like this could be used as the basis for a more finished studio picture, it is also quite satisfying as an end in itself.

sure to be part of it. In this way, you will keep the original proportions and sense of scale. It might even be worth passing through an intermediary stage of full size outline cartoon, on which you can think exclusively in terms of composition, and play about with the subject until you have achieved a satisfactory result in purely linear terms. Transfer this by rubbing over the back of the lines with soft pencil and tracing over, pricking through and mak-

ing an impression of the basic outline with pin holes, or anything else that occurs to you. Conversely, the square made on the final drawing can be used as part of the composition itself, as for instance in my views of Castle Howard or the Metropolitan Wharf at Wapping in London. If you don't want to draw over the sketch, use a sheet of acetate film with a grid drawn on it, which will work equally well for photographs. As your ex-

St Monance, a fishing village in East Fife, Scotland. 14" × 5".

perience grows your sense of composition will gradually become automatic.

For drawing in the details, the sketchbook and photograph are best used together. For colour slides, a back projector with a screen which sits on the table is invaluable, and obviously, this is the best sort of reference for transcribing colour. At other times black and white or colour photographs, coupled with a good sketch and vivid memory and imagination, prevent you from transcribing the photograph too mechanically. This is in fact how many well-known painters have worked, which is often surprising given the very loose and apparently formless paintings sometimes produced. Make your camera your servant, therefore, but do not become enslaved by it.

Many possibilities arise out of studio work, so do not neglect them. There might also be occasions when you are asked to work on a large scale for mural panels or special displays, when studio space is most valuable for handling large boards and for enabling you to step back and look at the work. Looking at your work upside down or in a mirror should not be despised, as you will thereby get a fresh understanding of its composition and tonal qualities. However, for all the fruitful possibilities of work in the studio, the initial sense of discovery in the field must never be lost; a return to the site of a subject can bring about a fresh and exciting viewpoint, and the artist must not deny himself this option by remaining enclosed in his studio.

Pictures for the Market Place

An artist specializing in the drawing of buildings is likely to find a number of commissions arriving for work which is not necessarily meant to be hung on the wall in a frame. You may find yourself working on a large mural, or on a small scale for book illustration, greetings cards or book jackets. All these types of work have their own rules and constraints, as well as offering exciting opportunities. If you have built up a sound technique by working in the field and practising at home, you will be ready to meet the challenge.

Murals need careful consideration. I was recently commissioned to paint one – for the offices of a yacht mart in Hampshire – to fill a long thin space. In this case, the river with which the business was concerned made an obvious subject. Over the 24 foot length I could show a variety of scenery which makes up the river bank. The key to success in a mural is to choose a subject which really fits the space it occupies, in all senses. It must be appropriate in subject as well as style, and make the best advantage of the quirks usually occurring in interiors, such as light fittings, door and window openings and corners. It is sometimes unfortunately necessary to tell a client that the small awkward poky room they had hoped to open up or disguise with a mural will actually look worse, however hard the artist tries to hide its faults.

It is as well, if possible, to paint a mural on panels or canvas away from the site, and fit it into place after the work is well advanced. In this way, you can prolong the short life of murals; when people and businesses move house they don't have to leave painting permanently on the walls which an unsympathetic successor is likely to obliterate – even assuming that you have been properly paid for your work, it is annoying to think of it being destroyed so soon. Panels also avoid the danger of damp plaster and flaking paint which can occur.

To gather the subject matter for the yacht mart mural, I walked up and down the river bank a great deal, and was rowed out into midstream by a boatman to sketch and take photographs. These notes were then made up to the right proportions, ready for submission to the directors. Sometimes this preparation can be more exciting than painting the mural itself and it might be good advice not to settle all the details too definitely at this stage, leaving yourself room for new developments while painting the finished work, and thus preventing it from becoming a tedious labour of transcription.

The surface in this instance was canvas, mounted with glue on panels of chipboard. Canvas on stretchers might have done equally well, but could be difficult to manage on such a large scale. Hard-

Big Pit Blaenavon at Gwent in South Wales. Like many of the coal mines in this area of Wales, the Blaenavon pit is no longer in commercial use. However it is being preserved as a working museum. 13" × 8".

Iron-Bridge. Spanning the River Severn between Coalbrookdale and Broseley in Shropshire, this is the first cast iron bridge erected in the world, its date, 1781, proudly cast on the side. It was built by Abraham Darby, and has traditionally been a popular subject for artists. 11" × 9".

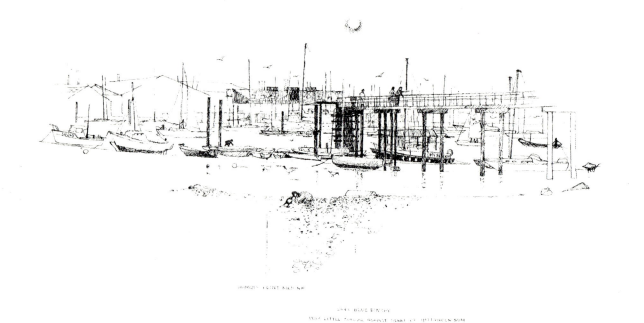

HAMBLE POINT MARINA

LOW TIDE DINGHY
VERY LITTLE MOVED AGAINST SLANT OF OUTRIGGER SUN

Preparatory sketches for a mural commissioned by a marine company with its offices in a yacht mart on the Hampshire coast at Hamble. I decided a good subject for the mural would be the yacht mart itself, and set about making nine drawings of the area, two of which are illustrated here (left and right, each measuring 14" × 7" and

HAMBLE POINT   FAWLEY   HAMBLE POINT MARINA   WARSASH JETTY

drawn in pen and ink on Saunder's watercolour board). In order to present the idea to the directors of the company commissioning the work, I made three watercolour roughs, drawn to scale, one of which is illustrated below. Also painted on Saunder's board, its three sections altogether measure 19½″ × 2¼″.

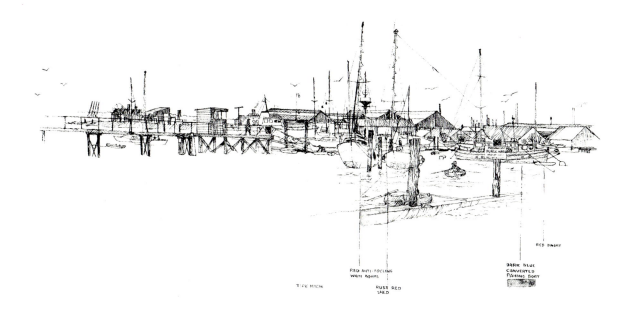

Houses on Arncliffe Green, in the Pennine hills in Yorkshire. Originally painted for the Abbey National 1983 Calendar, this watercolour is now in a private collection.

board primed on the rough or smooth side, according to choice, is another useful ground for mural panels. These surfaces can be used for oil, acrylic, or any of the other modern plastic based paints. In this instance I used vinyl co-polymer colours, which are sold in small pots. Eleven colours, cobalt blue, ultramarine deep, burnt sienna, burnt umber, violet, yellow, yellow ochre, orange, red, black and white, were enough for the needs of the subject.

As in watercolours, a disciplined palette and plenty of mixing gives a sense of wholeness to the finished work. The art of the great fresco painters of the Renaissance was to get the best out of their limited range of pigments, as well as working at speed on the wet plaster and cutting out inessential detail. Acrylic and vinyl colours seem always to be cruder than the traditional pigments and media, and murals can be done successfully in egg tempera and distemper (stage paint), where they are not going to suffer too much wear and tear. Oil paints would be another alternative, but unless you are used to their peculiarities, the new alternatives are certainly much easier and quicker to handle. They can be used, as I did in this case, in thin washes like watercolour, catching in the grain of the canvas.

A preliminary drawing was done in faint grey paint lines, and then washes of colour were built up, much like a watercolour, with areas such as the sails and boat hulls masked out to enable washes to carry straight over them uninterrupted. Apart from the change in the quality of the colour between the watercolour sketch and the full size work, the enlargement altered the compositional values, so that faults which were concealed before now needed to be compensated, particularly the shapes between objects. It was also difficult to keep the separate panels properly unified over such a large area, and most of the work had to be moved out into the garden to enable a distant view to be taken, which for a normal painting would have been perfectly easy.

The painting of Rovinj in Yugoslavia (pages 88–9) shows the development of a more abstract style which might be useful for abstract and decorative work. The town has fine eighteenth-century buildings showing Venetian influence, as is often found in Yugoslav and Greek ports on the Adriatic; but there is also a mediaeval city above it, perched on the hill of the peninsula. Its appearance as the evening sun slanted across the face of the buildings was extremely beautiful, the individual houses lost in the sense of the overall pattern. I sketched it from the quay with a limited palette, and took colour slides as the basis of a future painting.

When developing the subject at home, I chose a long shape, cutting out the tall church tower and concentrating on the vast wall of buildings facing the sea, familiar from all over the Mediterranean with their shuttered windows and ancient sun-burnt crumbling walls, fortunately surviving uninterrupted by modern hotels in this undeveloped place.

After a light pencil drawing, a mask of Frisk film was used to protect the main area of the houses, although the windows, some of the shutters, the roofs and the lines of washing were cut out to be exposed. The film acts as a stencil in reverse, and because it has a transparent backing, it can be fixed over the drawing and cut in place with the tip of a thin knife or scalpel, making sure that the blade does not cut down into the paper below. Once cut, the backing is removed and the film can be stuck down over the drawing. It was easier in this instance than the alternative method of using masking fluid, applied with a brush, which would be more suitable for irregular and small areas. Although the effect is in some sense mechanical, it is similar to many of the techniques of printmaking, and very useful at times.

The roofs were painted in with a warm mixture of burnt sienna and raw sienna, and parts of the windows and shutters with grey blue. The washing went in with small dabs of brighter colour. When the mask is peeled off, a lively coloured pattern is left, and this acts as a good basis for continuing to paint normally with details and light washes. If

Rovinj, Yugoslavia. The sketch of the medieval port with its Venetian inspired campanile right *was drawn across two pages of my sketchbook, the original measuring 22″ × 8½″. It was later used as the basis for the more stylized, almost abstracted, watercolour* above *which was painted in the studio.*

88

Opposite *Two illustrations for* The Good Hotel Guide, *Fox Amphoux in Provence, France above, and Castel Palace in Ireland below. Line drawings such as these can be easily and cheaply reproduced.*

The Bronte Parsonage at Haworth, in the Yorkshire Pennines. This fine early-nineteenth-century building, *with its distinctive stone quoins, is also interesting for its association with the Bronte family.*

part of the painting gets too strong in colour, it can go under the tap or alternatively a large brush can be taken lightly over the surface to lift off colour and give texture. The film can be replaced at any stage, even slightly out of place to give a double edge to the shapes and increase their abstract qualities. Succeeding sheets of film can be used over washes already painted underneath, so that a layered effect of sharp edged shapes is produced.

Book illustration is a great tradition which fortunately still thrives, especially in the field of children's books. Buildings make natural subject matter for a variety of books and I have worked recently on titles ranging from the *Good Hotel Guide* and *The London Cookbook* to *Travelling with a Sketchbook* and a number of articles of regional interest for *The Countryman* magazine. From the technical point of view of the printer, black and white line drawings in Indian ink are the cheapest and easiest to use, as they can always be printed with the type. Enlargements and reductions are fairly easy to make, but it is better to draw to actual size where possible to avoid unexpected distortion. You might also consider the possibility of using media like wood-engraving and scraperboard if you are likely to be doing much illustrating work, as these also give a clear black and white image, with added possibilities for expression.

Book jackets are less frequently drawn as illustration than they used to be, but I have enjoyed designing several. It is important to get a grasp of the content, setting and atmosphere of the book as your design will probably work its way into the consciousness of the readers, as well as having to help sell the book in the shop. The design must be

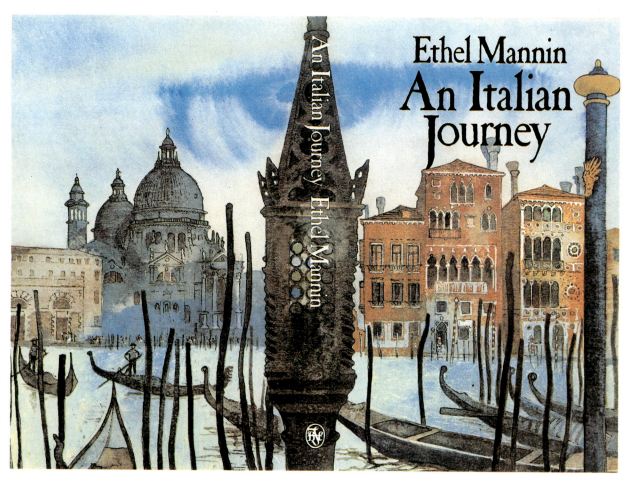

Ethel Mannin
An Italian Journey

An Italian Journey Ethel Mannin

Book jackets should be striking, and should evoke something of the character and mood of the book they are covering. Composition is particularly important, and special care has to be taken over the arrangement of lettering and the treatment of the spine of the book. The diagram, below, shows how the art work for the jacket of **An Italian Journey** would have been prepared.
The original measured 12" × 8¾".

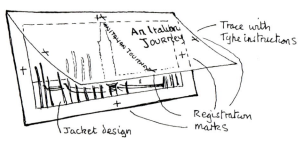

An Italian Journey

Trace with Type instructions

Jacket design

Registration marks

Unlike the jacket for An Italian Journey, *which was based on slides and sketches I had of Venice, the one drawn for* What Are The Bugles Blowing For? *uses an imaginary European city of my invention. Notice the different treatment of the spine: instead of being blocked off, it is made the focal point of the picture, with the marble stone paving leading up to a vanishing point half-way up it. The broad area of the square makes an ideal setting for the title.*

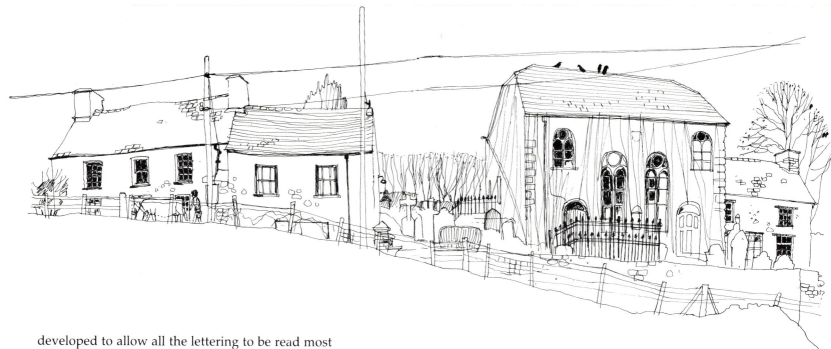

developed to allow all the lettering to be read most effectively, and the front, spine and back must have individual compositional value as well as working when seen together.

Draw accurately to scale and allow about an eighth of an inch all round for bleed where the printer will trim to make a clean edge. Fix a transparent overlay with the lettering layout, and specifications of typeface and size.

The bookjackets shown here were drawn in full colour for a four-colour process printing, which enables the intermediate tones and colours to be printed. Four-colour printing is the most commonly used method for printing colour nowadays and it is a good idea in choosing your palette to avoid fluorescent colours and colours such as gold

Pente-ty-Gwyn, Wales: 'Mrs Morgan fetches the morning milk'. The original sketchbook drawing (above) was adapted in the studio to make an attractive greetings card (right and above right). Although the shapes of the houses are closely copied, the tone values in the studio version have been treated with considerable freedom and an element of pattern and 'colour' has been introduced.

Mrs Morgan fetches the morning milk.
Pentre-ty-Gwyn
Ray Evans

Fold

4"

8¼"

Black line on a grey card.

and silver, which are impossible to reproduce by the four colour process. This will make the process of colour separation simpler and more accurate, hopefully leading to a more satisfactory printed result.

In approaching all these different types of painting and illustrating it is refreshing and stimulating to see how other artists have tackled similar problems. The great movements of twentieth-century art, like cubism, may seem remote from the sort of work you wish to do, but there is always much to be learnt about technique, improvisation and mixed media from an artist such as Picasso, while other purely abstract artists like Mondrian have much to teach about composition, or Matisse about colour.

95

Ray Evans
Grand Palace, Bangkok Dec. 1982

Buildings in Their Environment

The Grand Palace, Bangkok (15" × 10"). The exotic architectural detail on this complex of beautiful buildings meant that this watercolour with pen and ink took a good 4 hours. Painted on 140 lb. Bockingford paper.

Everyone with an interest in buildings will remember the moment when they suddenly became aware of what buildings mean. They are more than shelters, being full of the ideas and lives of the people who made them and lived in them, often over many centuries. We pass on, but they – if given sufficient care – will outlast many more generations and are worthy of our devotion, respect and interest.

My own interest in buildings dates from my childhood. I was brought up in Cheshire in England and I remember the excitement I felt in visiting Chester, with its many fine buildings encircled by the old Roman city wall. Chester also served as the gateway for expeditions further afield, into the country where my family originally came from, Wales. At fourteen I became the proud owner of a racing bicycle, and it was at that time that my lifelong interest in travelling began.

My first excercises in sketching came in the form of illustrated profile maps which I drew in the log books in which I recorded my cycling expeditions, which took me as far as ninety-two miles into Wales. In this I was not influenced so much by any of the great masters of the English watercolour school as by the work of an illustrator who worked for *Cycling Magazine* at that time, Frank Patterson. A cyclist himself, he drew countryside views which

nearly all contained architecture in various forms. His work instilled the habit of drawing in me, and also the outlook of the traveller, the arriver, the passer-by, whose interest is held while the drawing is made. I have already said that drawing a building is the only way of understanding it; to this should be added that one should not look at a building in isolation, but as part of the landscape in which you find it. In many cases much of the character of a building is derived from its environment, and the travelling artist should be very sensitive to this.

A good example of this is a building which I have known since childhood, the first to interest me as a subject. Known as the Shepherd's Hut, it stands on a small plateau about 1200 feet up on Cadair Idris. It was used by shepherds during the summer months when their flocks were out on the mountain, and it is typical of many such simple dry-stone buildings in the mountainous area of Snowdonia. It must be at least a hundred years since it was last in use, and today it is no more than a heap of stones, with one gable end still showing. The ghostly atmosphere of this ruin combines with the vast, bleak and stormy landscape of the mountains to create a subject with a very strong sense of place and mood. The large boulders which were used to build the Shepherd's Hut reflect the hostility of the climate on the mountainside.

97

Small clay
tiles.

The Kamthieng House,
Bangkok (8" × 6¼"). This
unique example of Northern
Thai residential architecture
is built on traditional lines,
using local materials.

98

Throughout my travels in Europe, Asia and the United States I have been particularly aware of how climate influences building, and how very often one can explain features of a building by asking what sort of weather it has been designed to withstand. Thus buildings in mountainous country are characterized by large overhanging eaves which are designed to protect them from the rain and snow, an annual and prolonged hazard. In Bangkok and Chiang Mai in Thailand I found that the need to survive in a very hot climate had led to beautifully proportioned wide, high rooms, with shades rather than glass over the windows. Similarly, there are the stone floors and shuttered windows of Mediterranean architecture. These factors, and the need to use local building materials, have all served to shape different styles of architecture around the world.

This is a particularly fine example of residential architecture in Chiang Mai. The typical broad eaves serve for protection against the rain and sun.

Mediterranean town life centres around the square; here, a port in Corfu. The church and tower are nice examples of late-fifteenth-century Venetian architecture.

Another factor I have always tried to bear in mind is the role of a building in its environment. This is equally true of the Shepherd's Hut and of St Mark's Cathedral in Venice; in both cases the buildings belong to their environment as they are fulfilling a specific purpose. Thus a farmhouse relates to its farm buildings and the agricultural land around it, just as in a Mediterranean town the church and cafes will both be found at the focus of town life, the square.

In the case of the more important buildings in town and country one should be aware of how they have created their own environment: for instance in Washington, buildings like the Capitol and the White House exist in a setting which has been created specially for them. In the English countryside this is particularly true of the great country houses. They are set in parks which were designed and literally sculpted by landscape artists, who sunk lakes, built hills and moved woods, all of which was of course done in the days when such vast projects were still within the means of the English aristocracy. The owners, though poorer, are still there, through their care preserving a sense of continuity which makes these places very attractive.

Hardwick Hall, as mentioned earlier one of the great innovative buildings of the Elizabethan period, is built on a ridge in Derbyshire, where its commanding position makes the cut out initials E S (for Elizabeth, Countess of Shrewsbury) on the parapet particularly effective. The massive bulk of the house against the sky is what fascinated me most and it was this monumental shape that interested me more than architectural detail.

Castle Howard is one of the great houses of York-

Hardwick Hall, 'more glass than wall', dominates the surrounding country with its imposing skyline. 9" × 7", drawn with a Pilot ball liner pen on smooth Wovex board.

shire, where things are done on a big scale. It hardly needed the television adaptation of Evelyn Waugh's *Brideshead Revisited* to make it more famous than it already was. It is a baroque palace designed by the playwright and soldier Sir John Vanbrugh, who had a strong feeling for the drama of buildings. As a subject for a painting, it seemed to me that there was no question of taking it at anything less than full length, although there was no natural position to sit and draw it in this way. However, the sheer length of the building contributes greatly to its immediate impact on the viewer, and in order to try to convey this effect I decided to use a long ribbon-like shape for my picture. This was painted from detailed drawings made on the spot, using a grid in order to ensure accuracy. The grid squares remain in the finished drawing, lending an abstract quality to the whole which unifies the composition and relates the building to the landscape around it. I used a very limited palette, with prussian blue, warm sepia, brown madder alizarin and raw sienna, adding a little new gamboge and black. I washed out and blotted frequently, using a large brush with plenty of water at first and finishing the picture by concentrating on the finer details. It was a fascinating exercise, in which I felt my way forward and let the subject dictate the method until I knew it was finished.

On a more modest level I have always been attracted by farms, and farm buildings from Connecticut to Provence feature in many of my sketchbooks. They have always struck me as eminently drawable because they fit into their environment so naturally, but always with some practical reason for their position: tucked into valleys for protection against the weather, by a river crossing, stream, or spring, on a drover's road or mountain pass. They belong where they are, are built of local stone or local timber and are completely functional. They are also attractive in that they represent the idyllic, healthy and rural alternative to town life; while working on a farm may be demanding, vis-

Below left *A huge barn in Pennsylvania (6½" × 4", drawn on bristol board in 20 minutes),* and below *Pen y Bont farm near the Black Mountains in South Wales (11" × 4½", pen and ink with wash, using a very limited palette). Both buildings seem to blend into the contours of the land around them.*

Right *farm near Plas Maenan in Wales (8" × 6", Rotring with wash on cartridge paper), and below White Farm near Senny Bridge, also in Wales (drawn in 30 minutes with B and 2B pencils on Bristol board, 8" × 4"). These sort of drawings are the result of happy discovery while travelling, and retain a sense of spontaneity and freshness which suits the informality of the subjects.*

Castle Howard

Castle Howard, Yorkshire, built by Sir John Vanbrugh.

Combourg, in Brittany; the Norman castle dominates the town below in an almost protective way. Drawn with a Pilot Hi Techpoint fibre tipped pen on French Canson paper in my sketch book; 8¼" × 5¼".

iting one on a fine summer's day can only be pleasurable. I made a watercolour of Maesgwyn farm in Wales on such a trip; the colour and shape of the hedge excited me, both being rather exaggerated but leading the eye to the delightful white farmhouse.

In Provence the whole landscape seems to be brought to life by the play of light and shade. The small village of Correns struck me as being very much like a farmyard. Its main street, shaded by great plane trees, serves as a daily route for cattle and farmers, who park their tractors by the village

cafe before setting off to the surrounding vineyards. The whole scene was very attractive and reminiscent of Van Gogh paintings.

Villages and towns, like farms, often owe their position to a river, and, more specifically, a bridge. Many communities grow up around bridges and ferries and these remain the centre of the community. Thus bridges provide fascinating subjects, ranging from simple stepping stones and foot bridges to those in the great cities, such as Tower Bridge in London or Brooklyn Bridge in New York. Here again one can appreciate how a structure's

The village of Correns in Provence. The southern, Mediterranean part of France contrasts sharply with the north. Normally lively, the streets of towns like Correns fall silent during the siesta hours of the afternoon.

106

PROVENCE 1980   Ray Evans

MAESGWYN
FARM
Ray Evans 9/5/80

Maesgwyn Farm, near Senny Bridge in Wales. Watercolour with pen and ink. The small white farmhouse stands out from among the surrounding trees and makes itself the natural focus for a picture.

Kingsand, on the Cornwall coast. The quick sketch (right, Rotring 0.5 pen on cartridge paper, 8½" × 2") was done in preparation for the watercolour below, commissioned for the 1983 Abbey National Calendar.

Ray Evans 81

A pack horse bridge in the Yorkshire textile town of Hebden Bridge. Drawn with HB, 2B and 4B Rowney Victoria pencils on cartridge paper measuring 6" × 4½".

appearance is related to its purpose: Tower Bridge, the centre of which opens to allow ships through to the old docks, is built like a castle not just to blend with the Tower of London nearby but also to suitably fulfil its role as the gateway to a great trading capital, as London was when it was built. At the other end of the scale there are the simple pack horse bridges to be found in the textile towns in the north of England; these were built for the mules and donkeys which carried wool down from the farms to the mills.

A type of bridge which is particularly striking is the covered bridge. I found many examples in the United States, the best of which are in Connecticut and Virginia. The purpose of covering a bridge like this is both to protect it from snow and prevent it

Another view of the pack horse bridge in Hebden Bridge, 6¾″ × 3¼″. The stone used on the buildings here is characteristic of this part of the Pennines.

A covered bridge near Essex in Connecticut. Drawn on rough Bockingford watercolour paper with B, 2B and 4B Conte-Gilbert Criterium 550 pencils, and then fixed with Rowney Perfix colourless fixative. 30 minutes, 6″ × 3″. Bridges like this are rarely found, and make particularly interesting subjects.

An original bridge with intricate decorative wood carving, at Wat Benjamabophit, Bangkok. Pen and ink, measuring 7½" × 6".

Opposite *The Villa cinema and supermarket, Bangkok.* Contrasting with the serenity of the Grand Palace, this Bangkok street scene from my sketchbook is no less exotic. Drawn with pen and ink, watercolour and gouache on a David Cox watercolour paper measuring 6" × 9".

from freezing over through frost. Subjects like this are all the more interesting for being associated with a particular country.

Often one is attracted to a subject by its historical associations. This is true of Harper's Ferry in Virginia, where some of the first shots of the Civil War were fired and, according to legend, 'John Brown's body lies a-mouldering in the grave'. The town lies on a spur of land between the confluence of the Shenandoah and the great Potomac, and strikes one as picturesque and unspoilt, reminding me of a Welsh mining village because of the many slate-roofed terraces of houses. The general store and other clapboard houses made very good subjects.

The skyline of a town can be its first and most striking feature to the traveller. This is perhaps most obviously true of New York, where the famous and breathtaking view of Manhattan from Brooklyn has been described earlier. This is just the most striking of many such views in New York – for instance around Central Park, or from windows in buildings themselves. I was immediately struck by the view from my hotel window (page 37).

Outside the big cities there are towns by the sea, with the buildings rising up from the waterfront, and these also provide striking skylines which make attractive subjects. The twin towns of Kingsand and Cawsand on the Channel coast of Cornwall are good examples. Kingsand, with its early twentieth-century water tower, red painted inn and cottages built up above the sea on ramparts, is very attractive; the shapes of these buildings dramatically silhouetted by the evening sun made a perfect subject.

Left *Harpers Ferry,
Virginia. Watercolour on
David Cox type paper in my
sketch book, measuring
8" × 7".*

Skylines and panoramas of
towns and cities make
striking and effective
subjects. Above right *the
skyscrapers of Manhattan
rise dramatically beyond the
winter trees of Central Park,
drawn in as much time as
the cold weather would allow
with a Rotring pen on
cartridge paper measuring
9¼ × 5".* Right *Salem,
Massachusetts, seen from
across its harbour on a
brilliantly sunny April day
and sketched in 2 hours on
watercolour paper measuring
18" × 6".* Most of the work
was done with No 6 and No
1 watercolour brushes using
a limited range of colours:
prussian blue, raw sienna,
brown madder alizarin, black
and warm sepia. Having
painted the subject without
any preliminary drawing, I
added a pen line in sepia
and black using a Gillott
303 nib, and this served to
strengthen the structure of
the composition.

Salem, Massachusetts, has many of the same qualities. Overlooking a dock with an old sailing ship is a skyline of pretty clapboard houses in smart clean but subtle pastel colours which look particularly attractive under a clear blue sky. While a practised artist can draw or paint anything, such subjects, with their qualities of shape, form and colour, translate naturally and easily into pictures.

Riverside and seaside views are equally interesting in cities. Amsterdam and Venice offer themselves as the two most famous examples of cities built on water, and the combination of water with architecture in these sort of settings has always attracted painters. Perhaps less popular is the industrial architecture of the waterfront. Nowadays in many city ports such as Boston and London fine

Amsterdam 1981 Ray Evans

Amsterdam: these tall houses are typical of the city, where land has always been expensive. This tradition of building tall was later taken up in a city the merchants of Amsterdam settled, New Amsterdam, later to be renamed New York.

116

Nineteenth-century industrial architecture has now reached an age which makes it both historically and stylistically interesting, nowhere more so than in the north of England where the Industrial Revolution was born. On this page, *above left* Piece Hall in Halifax, Yorkshire, drawn with HB and 2B Cumberland pencils. *Above* another view of Hebden Bridge nearby, and *below* a panorama of the town, set in a characteristic Pennines industrial landscape. On the opposite page, *far right*, a drawing with HB and 2B Cumberland pencils of Holdsworth Mill, showing the tall brick chimneys which are now largely redundant and threatened with demolition. *Right* miner's cottages in the old coal mining area of South Wales.

nineteenth-century warehouses have become redundant, but luckily there is a growing awareness of their particular beauty and many are being preserved. Such a building is shown in my painting of the Metropolitan Wharf at Wapping Wall, a warehouse in the old London docks which has now been restored and converted to house an art gallery, offices and a restaurant.

Industrial architecture as a whole has been long ignored, but recently there have been moves to preserve particularly striking buildings. This is true of industrial towns in the north of England, where railway societies, archaeological groups and local museums have worked to preserve the heritage of the industrial revolution. In drawing these towns I like using pencils of varying grades as the most suitable medium for drawing a grey and earthbound architecture, very much a part of the landscape surrounding it. Some of the Yorkshire mills

METROPOLITAN WHARF, LONDON 1981

The Metropolitan Wharf at Wapping on the River Thames, London. This fine nineteenth-century warehouse is typical of the many which lined the banks of the Thames when the Pool of London was the nerve centre of a great trading empire. Now that the docks have moved a good deal downriver to the estuary, many warehouses have been demolished. Some are, however, being preserved, like the Metropolitan Wharf which has now been converted to house offices, a restaurant and an art gallery, as well as retaining warehousing facilities. This highly finished studio picture in acrylics is given an abstract quality by the contrast between the colour wash applied diagonally across the face of the building and the squares of the grid used in order to scale it up from preliminary sketches.

Urban views are often incomplete without the crowds which give a sense of the bustle of town life. **Above** *Nabeul in Tunisia, a line drawing in black and brown ink (16″ × 5″).*

Right *a more familiar view, St Marks in Venice. This quick pen and wash drawing in my sketchbook (8½″ × 4″) takes in the famous features of the cathedral, campanile and Doge's Palace, surrounded by* *tourists and pigeons, in a form of shorthand. Unfortunately the prices at the bars around the square do not tempt one to stay much longer than the 35 minutes this sketch took.*

were built in an Italianate style and are fine and beautiful buildings with many delightful ornamental details. After legislation for fire-proofing was passed at the end of the nineteenth century, steel and reinforced concrete appear more. Although scenes such as these, or the mining valleys of South Wales, may not be obviously attractive, they are striking examples of how buildings and countryside fuse together to make a landscape with a strong individual character.

An aspect of drawing not yet discussed is the importance of depicting figures in pictures which include architecture. This has already been mentioned earlier in the book as a means of providing a gauge by which buildings can be measured. In drawing an urban landscape it is particularly important also to give a sense of life and activity which is essential to towns. It would be unchar-

acteristic to depict St Mark's Square in Venice without the pigeons and crowds of tourists which one will always find there. The concentration of buildings and bustle of life in towns has attracted me ever since my visits to Chester mentioned earlier, and features such as old city walls, defining the town and distinguishing it from the countryside are always worth looking for. City gates are particularly appealing as marking the meeting place between town and country, appearing both defensive and inviting.

All buildings have an individual character, and just as one only really properly understands the structure by drawing it, so too does one become aware of the purpose and place of that building. It is by recognizing the special individuality of your subject that you can hope to produce a satisfactory and even significant picture.

In old towns it is often the major medieval buildings which provide the focus of attention, and around which the newer parts of the town are arranged. This is particularly true of the buildings illustrated on this page. Below the Bargate, Southampton, parts of which are made up from the original Roman walls of the city. The gatehouse now incorporates a small museum. Drawn in pen and ink on cartridge paper.

Right Lincoln Cathedral, as seen from room 35 of the White Hart Hotel. During the hour and 20 minutes it took me to draw this tremendous view in my sketchbook (12" × 6"), the walls of the cathedral gradually changed colour in the light of the setting sun, until finally at dusk the floodlights were switched on.

Panoramic Paintings

Most of the paintings and drawings considered so far have been done from a single fixed viewpoint, but I have also mentioned how studio work enables you to develop from sketches, and give your subject matter the form which you think suits it best. When you come to do this, all your knowledge of building construction, and all your sketchbook notes will be of vital importance in helping you to re-interpret a distant subject in terms which are convincing and appropriate.

I have recently been discovering the delights of painting long panoramas of buildings, to give a flavour of the way a street or city unfolds over a long distance. It is something of the same effect of detached vision that is achieved with a *camera obscura*, mounted in a tower on a high point and projecting a natural image through lenses. This can still be experienced in the Outlook Tower near the entrance to Edinburgh Castle.

I was also influenced by the mediaeval paintings, where an architectural background enlivens the scenes going on in front, and is treated with the freedom which was possible before the discovery of fixed-point perspective. The frescos entitled 'Good and Bad Government' by Ambrogio Lorenzetti in the Town Hall of Sienna, Italy, are among the finest examples of this, and here the city itself is clearly the subject which most interested the painter. Although they were painted in the 1340s, they still reflect what Sienna is like now, with its narrow winding streets leading out into grand open spaces, and the hills visible outside the city walls.

A suitable subject for this sort of treatment was the waterfront at Dieppe, which gains in significance as the individual units of houses are grouped together, making an attractively varied outline. An additional advantage here was that not only was there a suitable viewpoint on dry land across the other side of the Bassin Duquesne, but there was also an excellent fish restaurant to help the work onwards, as I have recorded in the notes in the sketchbook. The study was done across two pages of a sketchbook on David Cox paper, which allows highlights to be worked up in white.

A different application of the same principle was a composite view of Winchester, based on sketches made from the top of St Giles' Hill, which commands a good general view of the town.

In the studio painting, the subject was elongated vertically, so that more could be squeezed in and the mediaeval sense of houses clustering round a great cathedral could be emphasized. In spite of the distortions of reality, a more intense idea of the city was conveyed, in a painting measuring thirty by twenty inches.

Waterfronts are particularly attractive for the lines of buildings overlooking the quaysides. The 20 minute sketch of Dieppe (right 8" × 6") was preparatory to the more highly finished view of the town from the Bassin Duquesne below. This was drawn on beige David Cox paper across two pages of my sketchbook (16" × 4"). My notes on the drawing describe how I began by drawing in the buildings in gouache, using white and raw sienna. I then moved to the roofs, painting them in black, prussian blue, warm sepia and brown madder alizarin. Pen and ink was used to draw in the details, and finally the foreground boats and masts were painted. Notes are always useful and interesting to have on one's drawings; in this case they end by recommending the Poisson Normande at La Maison du Père Tranquille, a restaurant by the cathedral!

Dieppe from the Chateau
4/8/80

I started by
painting the light areas
first, later blue grey roofs,
red roofs, finally a pen &
more white drawing.

time 1¼ hr.

It was a much more difficult problem to do the panorama which I thought would be an ideal treatment of the seafront at Aldeburgh, Suffolk. The beach shelves steeply in front, so that for sketches only a small piece can be seen at a time, and must otherwise be treated in perspective at a sharp angle. The effect of a shingle bank cutting off the houses abruptly was attractive and so were the fishing boats which punctuated the views at intervals. The houses are typical of the seaside with their pastel colours and different shapes of balconies, and I am determined to return and tackle the problem again, from an offshore boat, perhaps, or a pair of stilts.

In Amsterdam, things were very much easier. The chief feature of this wonderful city is the assembly of seventeenth-century houses along the canals which divide the city plan up into concentric rings. Because land on the canal frontage was very valuable, the houses are very narrow, although the plots extend back a long way behind. Thus a great variety of window shapes and gable designs can be experienced in a rapid movement of the eye, while the enjoyment of the buildings is enhanced by their fine brickwork and wooden sash windows, not unlike the seventeenth-century English William and Mary style.

Dieppe from the Chateau, a 1¼ hour drawing in one of my sketchbooks with a page size (8" × 5") corresponding to the Golden Mean. The lighter areas were drawn first with white gouache and mixtures of yellow ochre and white or brown madder and white. The darker blue grey and red brown roofs were then filled in, before finishing off the whole with pen and ink.

A characteristic Amsterdam street, drawn with a Rotring pen on cartridge paper (6½" × 6") for The Good Hotel Guide.

Buildings overlooking the Herengracht canal, Amsterdam. Drawn from a cafe in my sketchbook, the page measuring 8" × 5¾".

Only the Amstel River gives enough distance to get away from the buildings so as to get a natural panorama. The other canals, the Herengracht, the Keizersgracht and the Prinsengracht, are more attractive to walk along, but for the type of painting I wanted to do, a series of sketches and notes was necessary, shifting position from time to time. For the painting itself, a Saunders watercolour board was squared up and a careful outline drawing prepared in pencil from sketches and photographs. Over this I placed a carefully cut sheet of Frisk film, which protected the intricate gable shapes from accidental damage while the dark sky was being painted, and also helped to get a sharp dark outline for the door and window shapes.

The sky was painted onto paper which had already been dampened, using drops of acrylic magenta mixed with winsor blue, and in the centre, prussian blue with black. The same colours were used for doors and windows and because acrylic dries very rapidly I soon took off the film and put the board under the tap, blotting afterwards to produce more texture than is possible with a brush alone. After this, the sky was masked, and the first piece of film, for the houses, re-cut, to leave only houses which were white, or nearly so. With another wash which mixed acrylic magenta with raw sienna and warm sepia watercolour, the unmasked shapes of the houses were washed over. The mixture of two different types of paint gives an interesting texture.

The colour was dried, with assistance from the gas fire (matches and tapers are more selective) and it was once more put under the tap. The resulting pattern of shapes in different textured colours was very satisfactory, like the early stages of a lithograph. Despite the careful cutting, the freedom of the washes gives an accidental quality which would not occur in more conventional technique, where the edges of the drawing have always to be considered.

Because of the length of the painting it seemed sensible to follow the natural instincts of the human eye and concentrate on the detail in the centre, leaving the extreme edges rather indefinite. The work continued using the whole range of colours and brushes until it suddenly seemed finished. A cut mount placed over it helped to confirm this intuition.

The gable is perhaps seen in its greatest variety in Amsterdam, and the sketch, *right* only illustrates the basic generic types.

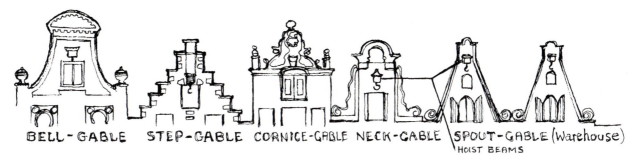

BELL-GABLE   STEP-GABLE   CORNICE-GABLE   NECK-GABLE   SPOUT-GABLE (Warehouse)
HOIST BEAMS

Below right *a pencil study using 2B and 4B pencils on Bristol board. Below a study with a Rotring pen of the street I later made a large scale studio painting of (pages 116–7). Masking with Frisk film, right is a useful technique to learn in applying colour washes.*

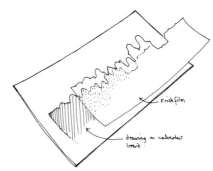

Frisk film

drawing on waterclear board

JEONG LOY   BOLS BAR HOTEL

The painting shown here originates from a 20 minute sketch and some photographs. Using these I squared up a piece of Saunders rough watercolour board and made a careful pencil outline drawing.

For my palette I chose Winsor & Newton watercolours: alizarin brown madder, raw sienna, and warm sepia in addition to prussian blue and ivory black. I used Winsor & Newton series 7 finest sable hair brushes and a 3" housepainter's brush.
Frisk film was fixed over the drawing and cut along the skyline of the buildings. The sky was then left masked while I washed over the

buildings with warm sepia, brown madder and raw sienna; while half dry this was washed out with the 3" brush. The process was then reversed, the buildings covered the sky washed in with water, the

dampened paper being easier to work with in applying a mixture of prussian blue and a touch of black. This again was washed out when half dry.
More detailed painting followed; trees, window frames, foreground railings, lampost and cyclist were all strengthened. Some whites were re-established on the buildings, either scraped out with a sharp knife, or by using a little gouache white.
Suddenly I realised that the picture was finished even though the detail was uneven at the edges. If I had carried on, I would have been guilty of overpainting and the spontaneity I felt the picture possessed would have gone. Although the drawing had been done the day before, the actual painting had taken little more than a further day.

Winchester: two versions of the same view, the first a preparatory study in pen and ink which takes in the main features of the city with a fair degree of accuracy. In painting the large scale studio picture (in acrylics) a certain amount of intended distortion takes place. The hills in the background are exaggerated slightly in order to close off the view and identify the boundaries of the city. The cathedral, as the main building of the city, has been increased in size so that it now dominates the composition. As a whole the composition has been concentrated and made more compact.

135

A panoramic view of
Aldeburgh, on the Suffolk
coast. This studio picture
was built up from a series of
field studies drawn on
Bockingford board. Far
right, drawn with a Rotring
pen in 35 minutes; right
drawn with 2B and B
pencils; and left a view of
the sea front houses from the
steeply rising beach, drawn
with 4B, 2B and B pencils.
In the watercolour above it
is interesting to note the
gable ends of the buildings
on the far right, an example
of the influence of Dutch
architecture from across the
North Sea common to East
Anglia.

Ray Evans

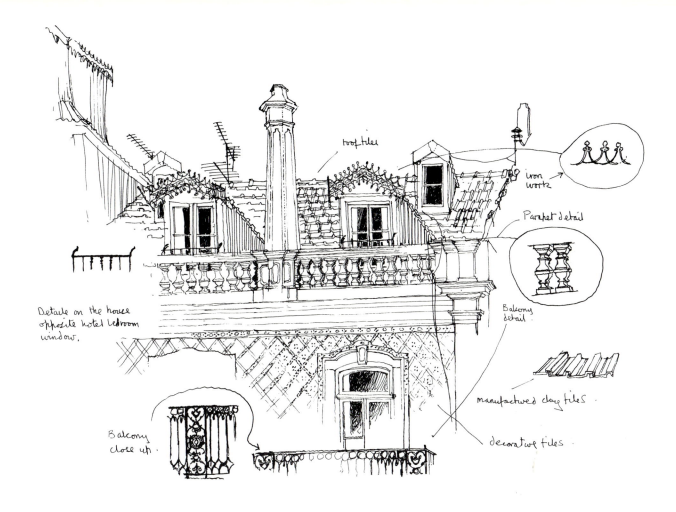

roof tiles

iron work

Parapet detail

Balcony detail

Details on the house opposite hotel bedroom window.

manufactured clay tiles

decorative tiles

Balcony close up.

Lisbon, Portugal: a panorama of the town looking out over the rooftops towards the bay. The pattern of the rooftops, and outline of the church against the sea beyond, makes this view particularly attractive. Drawn with a Rotring pen on cartridge paper, 11" × 6½".

Above *A Lisbon rooftop, drawn from my hotel bedroom. For me an essential part of travelling is the discovery of new architectural styles, and the decorative details on this rooftop made an interesting subject. Drawn with a Paper Mate felt tip pen on cartridge paper, 11½" × 8".*

The seafront at St Malo, on the Brittany coast. This large studio picture makes use of a similar composition and technique to my paintings of Amsterdam and the Metropolitan Wharf at Wapping (page 116–17 and 120–21). In finishing the pictures the use of a colour wash is particularly effective in giving a fairly accurate topographical work a certain abstract feel.

141

Below *A fine chateau at St Servan, near St Malo, drawn on a sheet of French Canson paper in my sketchbook measuring 8¼″ × 5¼″, using a Pilot Hi Techpoint fibre tip pen.*

St Malo, preparative sketches for the studio picture illustrated on pages 140–1. Above 2B and B pencils on Bockingford board measuring 5½″ × 4″. Above right also drawn on Bockingford board, here I used a uni-ball micro ball pen. 9″ × 4″.

This type of work is tremendously satisfying, provided that you have done the preliminary research on the spot. I could never have attempted the panorama of Lisbon without a mass of sketchbook information, about the strange and delightful methods of decorating balconies, pillars, dormer windows and towers.

The seafront at St Malo in France was a charming subject, full of reminiscences of Monsieur Hulot's holiday, with its small hotels and little boarding houses, mercifully uninterrupted by concrete monsters. The local Norman style of building with turrets and gables was adapted for these most unmilitary buildings, and here and there is an outbreak of crazy half-timbering, far exceeding the extravagance of the English south coast.

Unlike Aldeburgh, the beach here shelves gently away at low tide and presents a natural panorama. After work, what could be better than to face out to sea, for a change, with a dish of *moules marinieres* and a glass of muscadet, watching the sun go down?

143

BRIDPORT   SHAFTESBURY   WIMBORNE MINSTER   NEW FOREST

WEYMOUTH   LULWORTH COVE   POOLE HARBOUR   BOURNEMOUTH

A presentation rough for a mural decoration for a company in the south of England. The mural was made up of a series of scenes of local town and countryside views, and in order to present the idea these scale studies were mounted beneath card in two tones of blue-grey.

Presenting Your Work

Whatever form your work takes, if it is painted on paper or board it will need mounting and framing to show it off to best advantage.

Some painters have a rule – which one would like to follow – of never showing work to a prospective buyer or interested party of any kind, without putting it at least in a temporary mount. It is better still to cut mounts which suit the size and character of your picture.

It is easy to cut mounts to a nearly professional standard in the studio or the home without much special equipment, so here are some guidelines.

First, measure your picture carefully, with a long clear plastic rule, deciding exactly how large the centre opening should be. Choose the colour of mount which you think suits your own work best. I like grey or off-white mounts (not cream) with an inner slip mount in white. The double mount is a good device when working with any of the darker colours.

Decide how wide the border of the mount should be. For a watercolour of about ten by fifteen inches, it is best to allow two and a half to three inches all round and an extra half inch for the bottom of the mount, as an optical corrective to prevent the feeling which otherwise occurs, that the picture is lower than the centre.

Prepare a working surface, a table top or drawing

Cutting a mount: the three essential pieces of equipment are a heavy steel ruler, a strong cutting knife and a razor blade.

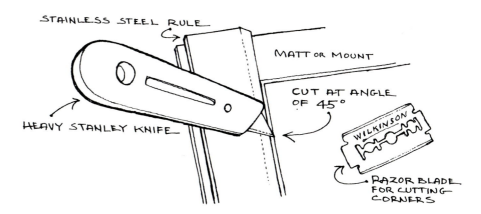

STAINLESS STEEL RULE

MATT OR MOUNT

CUT AT ANGLE OF 45°

HEAVY STANLEY KNIFE

WILKINSON

RAZOR BLADE FOR CUTTING CORNERS

The Dolphin Hotel, Southampton, seen here with the bombed remains of a medieval church in the background. Drawn with a Gillott 170 nib and india ink on CS watercolour board. Measuring 12 × 9½", this drawing took 1½ hours.

Right A composite view, including various Southampton scenes: the Hythe Ferry, Dolphin Hotel and the Bargate, shown on page 124.

DOLPHIN HOTEL

HYTHE FERRY

CANALWALK

Nº7 GATE
KOWLOON

PIER

Ray Evans
18·5·74

board on a stand, by laying down a sheet or two of millboard or strawboard, as a surface for cutting on. You will need a heavy knife with a sharp blade and a heavy steel straight-edge at least a metre long. Having decided on how much mount you are going to have, measure and mark the aperture lightly with a pencil. Use a tee square or a set square in order to make sure that the aperture is perfectly square to the whole. You are now ready to cut.

I prefer to cut from the face of the mounting card as this makes it easier to judge the 45° angle at which the aperture should be cut. Hold the ruler on the pencil line, clamping it if necessary, and cut along it with one long stroke, starting and stopping a little short of either end. When you have cut all four sides take a razor blade and gently cut each corner until the centre falls out. By this method you avoid an ugly cross mark at each corner.

Opinions differ as to whether you should cut the opening from the face or the back of the mount. The advantage of working from the back is that you can draw pencil lines wherever you like. The advantage of working from the front is that you can be sure that the knife is cutting cleanly.

Which way you chose may depend on whether you cut the opening with a Stanley or Utility knife, the traditional method, or take advantage of the specially designed American Dexter Mat Cutter (available also in the UK) which takes much of the effort and uncertainty out of mount-cutting, although it is not possible to achieve quite such good corners with it on heavier boards.

If you would like to make the effect more complete by adding a slip mount, tape a sheet of white mounting card over the back of the aperture, turn

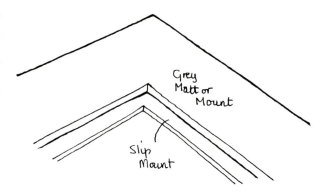

A slip mount used beneath a normal mount: contrasting colours can add to the effect of the frame.

it over and mark a margin of between one-quarter and one-eighth of an inch on the white card. Cut this as before. Sometimes I add a line or two of white on a grey card or pencil on white as a decorative effect. An architect's ruling pen or modern stylographic pen should be used if you want a coloured line. Another, but now old fashioned method, is to draw a wash line – two pencil lines filled with colour – round the aperture. Traditionally several such lines would be drawn on the mount, but considerable practice is needed to produce the required effect.

A customary sequence is to start with one or two dark but thin lines ruled nearest to the opening of the mount. Then comes the band of wash and then one or two more lines, getting thicker but lighter in colour. The lines and the band may be of different colours, related to the picture.

Draw your loaded pen along the upright (not the bevelled) side of the straight-edge, keeping it vertical and slightly away from the rule, to prevent smudging. Practise this operation a few times on a card off-cut before venturing on a proper mount.

For the band of wash even greater skill is required. Damp the area with a brush, taking care not to wobble. Then, with a saucer of dilute watercolour (tested for strength on a mount off-cut), take a wash swiftly and steadily round, taking as little time to reload the brush as possible and arriving back at the beginning before it has had time to dry. When the whole band has dried, rule round the inner and outer perimeter with a slightly stronger mix of the same colour.

This describes the basic techniques required for doing a wash line, and you will be able to observe from the work of other framers the many combinations of lines and bands which can be used.

Again, you may need the razor blade for finishing. The Dexter blades are very sharp, but after about six mounts they begin to lose their edge and should be replaced, so remember to buy a good stock of them. This is also true of Stanley knife blades.

It is not easy to make your own frames and this is not the place to embark on an explanation of how to do it. It would be best at first to find a good local framer and see which styles of frame best suit your work. Remember that frames are intended to protect your painting and therefore should not be delicate in themselves – plaster mouldings can break off very easily. Do-it-yourself metal frames are popular, though I prefer simple oak or gold with inset coloured lines.

Among more expensive frames, there are maple frames which lack the rich tones of the originals, but which could serve from time to time. 'Distressed' frames with their broken, rubbed or spattered texture are often very suitable and the conventional gold frame, if not too harsh, is always a standby. You will find that quality is expensive, but bad framing costs enough, so why not get it done as well as possible?

Beyond this it is probably best not to get too involved in framing; it is a specialized job and the time it takes could probably be more enjoyably devoted to painting. The essential quality which frames should have is to make it easier for your paintings to be moved around without being damaged. This is particularly important if you feel that you would like to start exhibiting your work. There is probably very little advice which can usefully be given here. It is obvious that you should start on the local circuit of exhibitions – in most areas there are exhibitions with an open submission. Contacts begin to build up and you will find commissions and offers to show your work arriving, if it has caught somebody's fancy.

People frequently ask for portraits of their houses or other much-loved buildings, which you may or may not execute, according to whether the client, subject and circumstances seem propitious. Keep a register of work sold so that you can build up a mailing list for exhibitions.

When handling and transporting framed pictures, take care to see that the corners are well protected as these are the most vulnerable part. In a car frames should always be stacked vertically and back to back, in the foot space of the back seat, for example. If sufficiently padded to prevent damage from violent motion, they will be perfectly safe like this (use old army blankets bought from government surplus stores).

In the studio, it is most useful to build a frame rack, of however rudimentary a kind, to get the

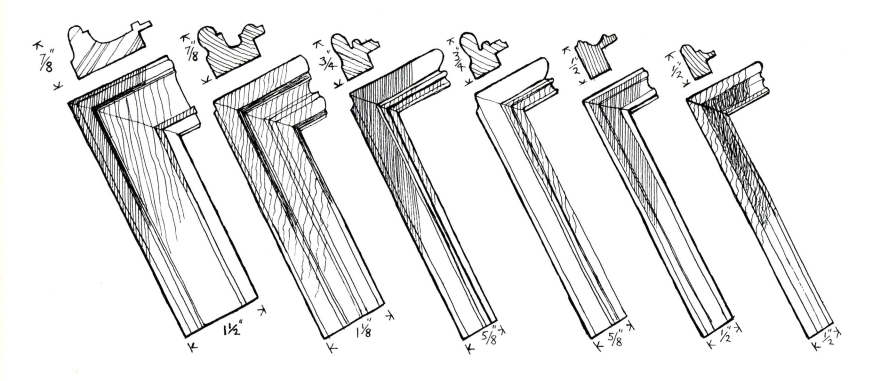

frames up off the floor and make them more easily accessible when visitors and clients arrive.

Artists are proverbially vague and unbusiness-like, but do not feel that this is a necessary professional affectation. If you are exhibiting or selling pictures, it is important to keep well organized records of all transactions and this becomes all the more necessary when dealing with mural commissions or graphic design work. Make certain at the onset whether the fee that you are being offered includes materials, transport, special fixing and any other costs which may make you out of pocket. After making a verbal arrangement, write a confirmatory letter and keep a copy.

Even if you are not a full time painter, a professional approach to your work will do good both to your own self-esteem and your public's image of you and your work.

150

Conclusion

This book has been addressed to beginners and experienced painters alike, to amateurs and professionals, if that distinction still has any validity. The main argument is in the pictures, as painting can only with difficulty be explained in words.

As far as words can manage, however, I would like to make a final plea. So many people say that they would like to draw or paint. Some form of artistic creation is well within the capacity of almost everyone with eyes to see and hands to work with. The difficulties are all in the mind, and it requires determination to overcome them. For complete beginners, there is the embarrassment of the childish appearance of the first efforts, but no painter will disdain these, and you have every right to consider yourself superior to non-painters in this respect. The process of building up a technique takes time and energy, and there is much frustration, and moments of temptation when it would seem to be much easier to give it all up. I do believe, however, that determination and imagination, which are part of the same thing, will carry anyone through.

These qualities become even more important when you have reached a certain level of competence. If painting is no longer a challenge to imagination and technique, it will begin to pall, both for you and your public. Take care what advice you take from people, who are always ready with suggestions which may lead you off the right track. A certain amount of bloody-mindedness, a determination to prove that your way is right, is always good for getting out of ruts. In any case, the only way in which work can progress is by continuing to work, and setting aside the many distractions of social and domestic life.

New materials, new places, and new subject matter all help from time to time. At other times, the same subject and the same materials, worked over repeatedly, will provide the way forward. Satisfaction is not easily won but there is no greater pleasure than producing work that you really feel is quite good, that is until the next time, when you think you can do even better, which is why dating and storing your work is so important: you will surprise yourself by your progress.

Glossary of Architectural Terms

Adze	A cutting tool with an arched blade which is set at right angles to the handle.
Arch	Curved structure of wedge-shaped bricks or stone.
Ashlar	Squared hewn stone, mainly used at quoins.
Auger	Carpenter's boring tool.
Baluster	A small shaped column.
Balustrade	A row of balusters supporting a rail of coping.
Batten	Small strip of wood to which slates, tiles, etc., are secured.
Bonnet tile	A curved tile used in hipped roofs.
Box-frame	Timber-frame construction used in building. In the USA this term is applied to window frames.
Brick bond	The pattern by which bricks overlap; brick courses are bonded like this for extra strength.
Brick nogging	An infilling of brickwork between timbers.
Camera Obscura	Dark chamber in which an image of outside objects is thrown onto a screen.
Casement	The case of a window frame; a window that opens on vertical hinges.
Ceramic	Any material, usually clay, shaped and then hardened by heat.
Chipboard	Reconstructed wood made of sawdust and wood trimmings, etc., consolidated with resin.
Clapboard	Weatherboard used as a cladding, usually on a timber-framed wall. Used first in East Anglia and later widely used in New England in the USA.

Classical	Style deriving from Ancient Greece or Rome.
Closer	A portion of an ordinary brick with the cut made longitudinally; also, the last stone or brick laid in a course, fitted to the opening so as to complete the row.
Cob	Composition of clay, straw and gravel used for building walls.
Cobblestone	Rounded stones or pebbles used as a crude building material.
Collar	A band around a column or other member, whether of the same or a different material.
Collar beam	A tie beam in a roof truss connecting two opposite principal rafters above the wall plate or foot of the truss.
Column	Vertical supporting pillar.
Coping	A protective covering on the top of walls to exclude water.
Corinthian	Third of the classical orders with acanthus-leaf design.
Cotton Gin	A machine for separating seeds from the fibre of cotton.
Cruck-frame	Two inclined vertical posts, sometimes curved, joined together at the top. Also called a crutch-frame.
Cupola	A miniature dome surmounted by a lantern or a small domed turret built upon a roof.
Doric	First and simplest of the classical orders.
Dormer window	Small gabled window projecting from a sloping roof.
Dress	To straighten, to flatten, to smooth.

By identifying and distinguishing the individual parts of your own home, you will become more aware of architectural detail in general. This drawing of my own house in Winchester highlights the main features which you should look out for when drawing buildings a Windows – sash, casement or with shutters? b Roof – varying in shape depending on the type of wood frame used to construct it; note also the type of tiles or slates which are used. c The eaves of the roof and guttering; pay attention to details such as the hopper head. d Specially shaped tiles such as ridge tiles along the top of the roof and bonnet tiles which lie on the end rafters.

e Chimneys often give a house much of its character, and can be a focal point for decorative brickwork. Note the variety of shape in pots which can be found (f). g Flashing – used around the chimney and other parts of the roof to protect against rain water. h Window surrounds are often picked out in stone or decorative brickwork, which is also used around the doors (i). Doors are themselves a fascinating subject, varying in style and contributing greatly to a building's character. j Walls can be made out of an infinite variety of materials, depending on their availability and local building practice. Here flint is used, while the rear extension has been rendered over with cement. k As is typically the case in flintwalling, the corners of the building are strengthened with quoins, in this case made out of brick.

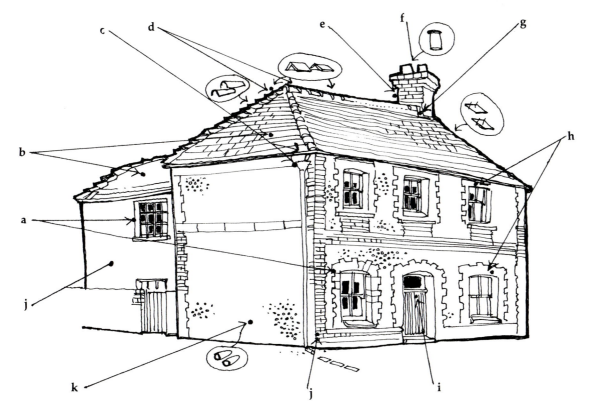

Dressed surround	Dressed stone jambs around windows.
Eaves	Lower edge of overhanging roof.
Edwardian	Characteristic of the style of architecture current during the reign of Edward VII (1901–10).
Fascia board	Long flat surface of wood under the eaves or cornice of a building.
Flashing	Narrow pieces of lead or other material required for water proofing at the intersection between vertical faces of walls and pitched roofs, flats or gutters, usually around chimneys.
Frog	Hollow in the top of a brick which acts as a key for mortar.
Gable	The triangular portion of a wall at the end of a roof.
Gambrel roof	The American version of the French double pitched Mansard roof.
Georgian	Term used to describe architectural style current during the reign of the first three Georges, from the accession of George I in 1714 to the beginning of the Regency period in 1810.
Glazing bars	Vertical or horizontal bars dividing a window.
Half timbering	Form of building in which the main structure is of timber with infilling of wattle and daub, brick or stone.
Hall house	A large open halled timber-framed medieval building.
Hammer beam	Beam projecting horizontally from the top of wall but not meeting across to members opposite.
Header	Brick end.
Herring bone pattern	Infill of bricks laid diagonally.
Ionic	The second of the classical orders.
Jacobean	Term used to describe the style of architecture current during the reign of the Stuarts (17th century).
Jamb	Side post of a doorway, window, fireplace etc.
Joists	Bearing timbers, floors and ceilings.
Jettied construction	Floor beams cantilevered outwards to provide a base for projecting upper storey.
Knapped flint	Cobble snapped across and dressed (knapped).
Lacing course	A continuous course of long thin stones or bricks at intervals in a flint wall.
Lath	A thin narrow strip of wood.
Lath and plaster	Split laths nailed close together so that the thick plaster would penetrate the gaps and spread behind them.
Lintel	A member of wood, stone or concrete placed horizontally to support the structure above an opening.
Mansard roof	A double pitched roof.
Mathematical tile	An English device, also known as mechanical or brick tiles, shaped to imitate the header or stretcher of a brick.
Mullion	Vertical tracery in a window.
Palladian window	Arch on twin columns flanked by flat headed windows.
Pargetting	Moulded decorative patterns, worked into wet plaster.
Pediment	Triangular gable above door or window.
Piazza	An Italian square. Also, the old-fashioned term for a long verandah on the side of American colonial houses, mainly in North and South Carolina.
Pisé	Rammed earth construction.
Plinth	Projecting base of stone or brick at the bottom of walls or pillars.
Portico	Colonnaded entrance to a building.
Purlin	Additional horizontal member to support rafters in the roof.
Queen Anne	Characteristic of the style of architecture current in the reign of Queen Anne (1702–14).
Quoin	Cornerstone on the angle of a wall.
Rafter	Similar to joist but inclined.

Regency	Elegant style of architecture when George, Prince of Wales was Regent (1810–20).
Rendering	Waterproof finish to wall surface such as cement, lime and sand.
Ridge	The highest horizontal timber of the roof to receive the heads of the rafters.
Rose window	Circular window with radiating tracery.
Silo	Airtight tower for storage of grain or winter food.
Stretcher	Long side or edge of a brick.
Stucco	Plaster or cement used as low relief decoration, also applied to the whole façade.
Tudor	Characteristic of the style of architecture current during the reign of the Tudors (16th century).
Victorian	Characteristic of the period ca. 1837–1901.
Wall plate	Wood members to serve as bearers for joists.
Wattle and daub	Interlaced rods of twigs which are plastered over with mud or clay to make a wall.
Wooden shingles	Slip of wood used as a roof tile or as siding.

Bibliography

Badmin, S. R. *The British Countryside in Colour* Odhams Press, London 1950.

Betjeman, John, and Piper, John, eds. *Murray's Architectural Guides* (Buckinghamshire 1948, Berkshire 1949, Lancashire 1955) John Murray, London.

Shell County Guides Faber and Faber, London.

Betjeman, John *A Pictorial History of English Architecture* John Murray, London 1972.

Billcliffe, Roger *Mackintosh Watercolours* John Murray, London 1978.

Borgman, Harry *Drawing in Ink and Drawing for Reproduction* Watson Guptil, New York 1977.

Briggs, Martin S. *Everyman's Concise Dictionary of Architecture* J. M. Dent, London, E. P. Dutton, New York 1959.

Brunskill, R. W. *Vernacular Architecture, An Illustrated Handbook* Faber and Faber, London 1978.

Butlin, Martin *Turner Watercolours* Barrie and Jenkins, London 1970.

Casson, Sir Hugh *Hugh Casson Diary* Macmillan, London 1981.

Clifton-Taylor, Alec *The Pattern of English Building* Faber and Faber, London 1978.

Six English Towns, Six More English Towns BBC, London 1979 and 1981.

Dixon, Roger and Muthesius, Stefan *Victorian Architecture* Thames and Hudson, London 1978.

Downer, Richard *Drawing Buildings* Studio Drawing Books, London 1962.

Fleming, John, Honour, Hugh and Pevsner, Nikolaus *The Penguin Dictionary of Architecture* Penguin Books, Harmondsworth 1966.

Fletcher, Sir Bannister *A History of Architecture on the Comparative Method* Athlone Press, London, Scribners, New York 1961.

Gentleman, David *David Gentleman's Britain* Weidenfeld and Nicolson, London 1982.

Gibberd, Frederick *The Architecture of England* The Architectural Press, London 1945.

Gill, Robert W. *Basic Perspective* Thames and Hudson, London 1974.

Harris, Cyril M. *Historic Architecture Sourcebook* McGraw-Hill, New York 1977.

Harris, John, and Lever, Jill *A Glossary of Architecture* Faber and Faber, London 1966.

Hilling, John B. *Cardiff and the Valleys* Lund Humphries, London 1973.

Hofer, Philip *Edward Lear as Landscape Draughtsman* Harvard University Press and Oxford University Press, 1967.

Hogarth, Paul *Drawing Architecture* Watson Guptil, New York, and Pitman, London, 1973.

Jones, Barbara *Watercolour Painting* A & C Black, London 1960.

Kelly, Frederick *The Early Domestic Architecture of Connecticut* Dover Publications, New York 1963.

Kutcher, Arthur *Looking at London* Thames and Hudson, London 1978.

Lancaster, Osbert *Progress at Pelvis Bay* John Murray, London 1936.
Draynflete Revealed John Murray, London 1954.
Here of all Places John Murray, London 1959.
Scene Changes John Murray, London 1978.

Lloyd Wright, Frank *Three Quarters of a Century of Drawings* Academy Editions, London 1977.

McKay, W. B. *Building Construction* Vols I–IV Longman, London and New York 1938; constantly reprinting.

Nuttgens, Patrick *The Mitchell Beazley Pocket Guide to Architecture* Mitchell Beazley, London 1980.

Patterson, Frank *The Art of Frank Patterson* CTC, London 1979.

Peel, J. H. B. and Maddox, Ronald *An Englishman's Home* Cassell, London 1972.

Pevsner, Nikolaus *An Outline of European Architecture* Penguin Books, Harmondsworth 1943.
The Buildings of England (by county) Penguin Books, Harmondworth 1950–.

Philip, Raymond 'The Architectural Drawings of Gordon Cullen', *Image* 8, Summer 1952.

Prizeman, John *Your House, the Outside View* Blue Circle, Hutchinson, London 1975.

Rasmussen, Steen Eiler *Experiencing Architecture* M.I.T. Press, Cambridge Mass. 1978.
Towns and Buildings M.I.T. Press, Cambridge Mass. 1979.

Richards, J. M. *The Functional Tradition in Nineteenth Century Industrial Building* Architectural Press, London 1956.

Risebero, Bill *The Story of Western Architecture* The Herbert Press, London 1979.

Rowntree, Kenneth *A Prospect of Wales* Penguin Books, Harmondsworth 1950.

Searle, Ronald and Webb, Kaye *Looking at London* News Chronicle, London 1953.
Paris Sketchbook Saturn Press, 1950.

Service, Alistair *Edwardian Architecture* Thames and Hudson, London 1977.

Sloane, Eric *The Age of Barns* Ballantine Books, New York 1974 and 1979.

Stamp, Gavin *The Great Perspectivists* Trefoil Books, London 1982.

Thelwell, Norman *A Millstone Round My Neck* Eyre Methuen, London 1981.

Unrau, John *Looking at Architecture with Ruskin* Thames and Hudson, London 1978.

Walcot, William *Architectural Watercolours and Etchings* Technical Journals, London 1919.

Wang, Thomas C. *Sketching with Markers* Van Nostrand Reinhold, New York 1981.

Watkin, David *English Architecture* Thames and Hudson, London 1979.

Wilkinson, Gerald *Turner's Colour Sketches 1820–34* Barrie and Jenkins, London 1975.

Wyeth Andrew *The Art of Andrew Wyeth* New York Graphic, Boston 1973.

Beyond this large general list it is worth looking out for local guide books, particularly walking tours which will usually include information on the history of individual buildings. These are too numerous for a full list to be included here, but it is worth mentioning individual books I found useful on the travels described in this book:

Colonial Williamsburg Official Guide Book, Williamsburg 1981.

Hogarth, Paul *Walking Tours of Old Boston* Brandywine Press, E. P. Dutton, New York 1978.
Historic Houses, Castles and Gardens in Great Britain and Ireland ABC Historic Publications, London, annually.

Iseley, Jane, and Davis, Evangeline *Charleston Houses and Gardens* Preservation Society of Charleston, 1975.

Koring, Hans, and Ward, Patrick *Amsterdam* Time Life Books, Amsterdam 1977.
Legacy from the Past A Porfolio of 88 Original Williamsburg Buildings. Williamsburg, 1978.

Madden Ross, Corrine, and Segaloffe *To Market, To Market* Six walking tours of Old and New Boston. Charles Rivers Books, Boston 1980.

Index

Figures in italics indicate illustrations.

book illustrations 91
book jacket design 91, *92–3*, 94
brick 10, 12, *15*, 19, *21*, *24–5*, 152
bridges 106, 110, *111*, *112*
brushes 54, *55*

clapboard 18, 30–31, 152
clay tiles 12
Coade stone 18
cob 14, 152
colonial architecture (American) 29, 32, 34
colour, use of 42, 72, 76–7, 132–3; *see also* paints
composite pictures *147*
composition 38, 39, 49–50
country houses 100–102, *104–5*
Cox, David, *see* paper

drawing methods 8–9, 30–31, 50, 64, 69, 76–7, 87, 123, 130–31
doors 26, *27*
dry-stone construction 14

easels *51*, *61*, 62–3

exhibiting work 150

farms 102, *103*
fascia board 12, 154
fieldwork 7, 62–3, 64, 69, 97
flintwalling 10, 12
frames *149*, 149–50
Frisk film *see* masking

gables 129–30, *131*, 154
grid, use of 46, *47*, 78–9, 101–2, *132–3*
golden section *see* composition

industrial architecture 115, *118*, 119, *120–21*, 123

jambs 12, 154

lath and plaster 10, *13*, 154

masking *44*, 87, 130, *131*
mathematical tile 18, 154
metalwork 19, 22, *139*
mounts *144*, 145, 148–9
murals 81, 84–5, *144*, *147*

paints 54, *55*, 86–7

panoramic views 126, *127–8*, *134–5*, *138*
paper *53*, 57, 60, 62
pargetting 14, 154
pencils 51, *52*
pens 51, *52–3*, 54, *55*
perspective *42*, 43, 46–7, 49
piazza 32, 154
pisé de terre see rammed earth
purlins 12, 154

quoins 10, 12, 14, 154

rafters 12, 155
rammed earth 14, *28*, 29–30, 154
roofing techniques 18–19, *21*

shingles 18, 155
sketchbooks *see* paper
skyscrapers 34, *35*, 36, *37*
stone 14
studio work *58–9*, 72, 78–80, *132–3*

wall plate 12, 155
windows 10, 13, *21*, *22–3*
wood frame construction 13, *16–17*, *21*, 34